DEVON AND CORNWALL RECORD SOCIETY
New Series, Vol. 22

DEVON AND CORNWALL RECORD SOCIETY

New Series, Vol. 22

TUDOR EXETER

TAX ASSESSMENTS 1489–1595

INCLUDING THE

MILITARY SURVEY 1522

Edited by

MARGERY M. ROWE

East Devon Area Archivist

Printed for the Society by
THE DEVONSHIRE PRESS LTD.
TORQUAY

1977

CONTENTS

CONTENTS

INTRODUCTION

The documents printed in this volume were selected by Professor W. G. Hoskins from taxation records surviving in the Exeter City Archives in the East Devon Record Office and in the Public Record Office, with the intention of providing a companion volume to *Exeter in the Seventeenth Century: tax and rate assessments 1602–1699*, which he edited for publication by the Devon and Cornwall Record Society in 1957. The eight records published in this present volume give lists of Exeter's taxpayers and the sums paid by them to the Crown at various dates between 1489 and 1595 and reflect the differences in the structure of taxation and the bases of assessment which occurred between those dates. Taxation records contain pitfalls for the historian and the poor condition of some of the documents here transcribed, especially the subsidy assessment of 1524, has made interpretation more difficult. Nevertheless they are of use to the economic historian for a comparative study of different towns and regions, and also to the genealogist, for the fullest of these returns, the Military Survey or Muster of 1522, antedates the earliest parish registers by at least sixteen years.[1] All except the first document in this volume, the ' Tenth ' of 1489, are arranged by parish, and therefore give information on the mobility of population into and within the City during the sixteenth century, a time of economic expansion for Exeter.

THE ' TENTH ' OF 1489

In January 1489 Henry VII obtained from Parliament the grant of a subsidy which differed from previous subsidies in that it was a combination of the usual medieval ' fifteenth and tenth ' and an extra tax on land and income. In the case of boroughs such as Exeter, the supplementary tax was to be levied at the rate of ten per cent on income from land together with 1s 8d on every ten marks' worth of movables in excess of ten marks, but because the total levied throughout the country did not produce the required sum for the waging of Henry's war in Brittany, it was necessary to reinforce it with a ' fifteenth and tenth ' levied on personal goods (movables). This rather complicated basis of assessment produced the first tax on both realty and personalty that was actually levied.[2]

Apart from occasional new taxes such as the Poll tax, first levied in 1377, the basis of taxation from 1334 and up to 1489 had been the fifteenth and tenth—the fifteenth applying to rural areas and the tenth to the boroughs and ancient Crown demesne—and the Crown negotiated on a collective basis for a payment from each tithing, hamlet, borough or demesne. The payments were based on a valuation of 1334 and as the only attempt to make the ' fifteenths

---

[1] See Appendix II.

[2] James Tait (ed.), *Taxation in Salford Hundred 1524–1802*, Chetham Society, new series, 83 (1924), p. xxiv. ' An Acte for a Subsidye graunted to the Kyng ', 23 February 4 Henry VII cap. 20 is printed in *Rotuli Parliamentorum*, VI, pp. 420–4.

and tenths.' more realistic consisted of a series of tax abatements, by the end
of the fifteenth century the sums collected by this method were far from satis-
factory. [1] Thus the assessment in 1489 represented a departure from the usual
tax on movables. The assessment was to be made by royal Commissioners and
the collectors were to be appointed by them. The collectors were to value the
property of the inhabitants, and when the assessments had been scheduled they
were copied and indented. The chief collectors then conveyed the money or a
greater part of it to the Exchequer with one copy of the indented schedule and
they retained the other themselves in order to complete the collection.

The assessment of the lands and goods of Exeter's inhabitants is dated 7
March 1489 and the copy of the list which is here transcribed names twelve
collectors for the City. This list was discovered with other local copies of tax
assessments in the Exeter City Archives [2] and is the only surviving copy.
Indeed, few local copies of this particular assessment survive in local records or
in the Public Record Office and none has been printed. [3] The Exeter document
is a long roll, now approximately eleven feet long but torn at the foot, and the
membranes are bound Exchequer fashion. The last three feet are badly
stained and the preceding two feet eaten away at the left hand edge. Nevertheless some four hundred and fifty entries can be distinguished and each of these
gives the name of the inhabitant and whether the payment is made by one
person (by the hands of) on behalf of another or for himself, the former presumably indicating that the person liable was simply the tenant and not the
owner of the property. Unlike most of the later assessments printed in this
volume, only one figure is given, which purports to represent the tenth part of
the property owned by each inhabitant, plus a levy of 1s 8d on every ten marks'
worth of goods above ten marks. It is not possible to discover from the roll how
much the collection brought in as it is incomplete and the final account of the
collectors for Devon gives the sum total of receipts less expenses from the whole
county. Totals for individual boroughs are given in the assessment made in
1489–90, however. [4] The amount raised from the country generally proved to
be insufficient: two years later Parliament granted to Henry VII another
subsidy of a fifteenth and tenth and this time no supplementary tax was added. [5]

The Exeter roll for 1489 gives valuable information as to the names of what
must be a fair proportion of the City's wealthier inhabitants and apart from a
Murage Roll of *temp.* Edward III [6] is the fullest list of Exeter's inhabitants that
survives in the Exeter City Archives before 1500. Unfortunately the list is not
divided into wards (as is the Murage Roll) or parishes, as are the later subsidies. Nevertheless, it is possible to identify a few parishes approximately.
The record probably begins with the parish of St. Lawrence as the Wardens of
that parish appear early in the list and St. Petrock's parish may also be identi-

[1] Audrey M. Erskine (ed.), *The Devonshire Lay Subsidy of 1332*, Devon and Cornwall Record
Society, new series 14 (1969), p. ix; W. G. Hoskins, ' The Wealth of Medieval Devon ' in
Devonshire Studies (1952), pp. 212–49.

[2] East Devon Record Office, Exeter City Archives, pressmark Z6. Hereafter documents in the
Exeter City Archives are cited as E.C.A.

[3] E. L. C. Mullins, *Texts and Calendars : an analytical guide to serial publications*, Royal Historical
Society, 1958.

[4] Public Record Office, E.179/95/127 and 128. The latter document is the final account of
the Devon collectors and gives the sum total of receipts less expenses. The totals for individual
boroughs raised in the assessment of 1489–90 (E.179/95/127) are given in W. G. Hoskins, *op.
cit.*, p. 247.

[5] *Statutes of the Realm*, II, pp. 555–6, which cites the Act as 7 Henry VII cap. 11.

[6] E.C.A., Miscellaneous Roll 72.

fied. However the arrangement may well have been under the name of the owner rather than according to where the property was situated as usually blocks of property belonging to the same person are listed together, or it is possible in at least some cases that an owner held a row of houses in one block rather than houses scattered throughout the City. This may be evidence for extensive house building in the City in the second half of the fifteenth century, allied with the considerable growth in trade and the changes in the City's government in the late-fifteenth and early-sixteenth centuries, but the roll of 1489 can provide no definite pattern of land tenure in the city. No tenements of the Mayor, Bailiffs and Commonalty of the City of Exeter are listed although it is known from the series of Receivers' Rolls, almost complete for the late fifteenth century, that a considerable amount of property was owned by them, most of this rented out. The general impression is that there were very few property owners in Exeter, although it is not possible to be certain about this because of the incompleteness of the roll. By a comparison with the admissions to the freedom of the City[1] and with the series of deeds in the Exeter City Archives, the names of those persons which are given may be verified as being 'substantial' persons.

THE MILITARY SURVEY OF 1522

During the early years of Henry VIII's reign unexpectedly heavy war expenditure in France and Scotland had been incurred. The deficiencies of the medieval taxation system based on the fifteenth and tenth have been discussed in so far as they concerned Henry VII's reign and although this method of assessing taxes was still in being in his son's reign, the sums raised were disappointingly small. A new system of raising cash was required and one which made certain that all the wealthier members of the community would be included, for the old system of raising taxes had been largely in the hands of local assessors who had themselves often escaped with a reduced assessment. A valuation of the whole kingdom was attempted by Wolsey in 1522. This may be considered the most ambitious since Domesday Book or the Hundred Rolls of 1279 and it is more comprehensive than either. This new valuation was obtained by Wolsey by subterfuge, under the guise of a Muster or Military Survey.

The Statute of Winchester of 1285 required all men with £10 in lands or 20 marks in goods to keep a complete set of armour, while those with £15 in lands or 40 marks in goods were also to keep a horse, and this method of raising troops for national defence was still in being in the Tudor period, and at intervals when they were held in their particular county men were required to attend musters with their accoutrements. In practice they would probably not have attended in person and the provision of armour in the Tudor period became the responsibility of the town, parish or hamlet, as is witnessed by the sums spent on this appearing in Churchwardens' accounts. At the musters held in the counties Muster Commissioners, with the Constables, were required to inspect the harness, see that an assessment was made of each man's quota of the costs to the locality, and then to draw up the appropriate muster certificate. In March 1522 Commissions were issued and in addition to the customary returns of able-bodied men, arms and harness, the constables were

---

[1] Margery M. Rowe and Andrew M. Jackson (eds.), *Exeter Freemen 1266–1967*, Devon and Cornwall Record Society, extra series I, 1973.

on this occasion to certify in writing the names of all men above the age of sixteen ' and whom they belong to '. They were also to certify ' Who is the lord of every town and hamlet . . . who be parsons of the same towns and what the benefices be worth by the year . . . also who be the owners of every parcel of land within any town, hamlet, parish or village . . . with the yearly value of every man's land within the same '. Aliens or strangers who lived in the towns were to be listed, with their place of birth and their occupations and the return was to include also a note of every man's goods, spiritual as well as temporal. Finally, it was to be specified ' what pensions goeth forth out of any land there to any religious or spiritual men '.[1]

Evidently the manner in which these instructions were carried out was un-satisfactory as more were sent out in July 1522 requiring the Commissioners to repeat the financial part of their surveys. When the enquiry was complete the commissioners were to call together ' suche temporall personages as they shall think good ', explain the King's necessity in the present state of war with France and Scotland, and all those with property worth £20 or more were to be asked to loan money to the king at the rate of ten per cent or above. New survey books were compiled in the late summer and early autumn but it is not possible to say when these were completed.[2] Twenty-nine counties are known to have sent in complete returns,[3] but very few of these survive in the Public Record Office or indeed, elsewhere,[4] and the local copies vary in the information they contain.

The returns made for only two boroughs survive: the Military Survey of 1522 which is published in this volume and the Muster Certificate Book in the Coventry City Archives.[5] The Coventry volume differs slightly from the Exeter one in that it arranges the information given in the survey by ward but rents of leasehold premises, valuations of freehold premises, valuations of personal property and details of weapons and armour are listed in a similar way to the Exeter valuation. As well as the Coventry Muster Certificate Book, other lists of householders for certain streets in Coventry survive for this date, and these lists include returns for women and children.[6] The Exeter survey lists the information under fourteen of the city parishes in addition to the Canons

[1] The instructions issued by the Commissioners for Essex to the bailiffs and chief constable of the half hundred of Waltham are printed in John Stow, *Annals* (1621), p. 515 (his original is British Museum Stowe, 570, fo. 165). For a similar appointment of Commissioners in War-wickshire see *Letters and Papers of Henry VIII*, iii, 2484. For information on the 1522 muster and these instructions see Julian Cornwall, ' A Tudor Domesday ', *Journal of the Society of Archivists*, III, no. 1 (April 1965), pp. 19–24; J. J. Goring, ' The General Proscription of 1522 ', *English Historical Review*, LXXXVI, no. 341 (October 1971), pp. 681–705; A. C. Chibnall, *The Certificate of Musters for Buckinghamshire*, H.M.S.O., 1973. For information on Tudor Musters see Jeremy Goring, ' Social Change and Military Decline in mid-Tudor England ', *History*, vol. 60, no. 199, June 1975, pp. 185–97. Two further articles by Julian Cornwall also contain a discussion of the 1522 Muster. These are ' English Country Towns in the 1520s', *Economic History Review*, 2nd series XV, no. 1, August 1962, pp. 54–69 and ' English Population in the Early Sixteenth Century ', *ibid.*, XXIII, no. 1, April 1970, pp. 32–44.

[2] J. J. Goring, ' The General Proscription of 1522 ', p. 687.

[3] *Letters and Papers of Henry VIII*, iii, 3683.

[4] For lists of surviving returns see J. Cornwall, *Society of Archivists' Journal* and J. J. Goring, ' The General Proscription of 1522 ', p. 687n.

[5] Coventry City Record Office, Accession 24. I am indebted to Mr. D. J. Rimmer, Coventry City Archivist, and to Mr. C. Phythian-Adams of the University of Leicester, for information on the Coventry 1522 Muster. Mr. Phythian-Adams hopes to publish an analysis of the contents of the volume.

[6] Coventry City Record Office, Accession 263.

of the Cathedral Close. Only the parishes of St. Lawrence, St. Mary Steps and All Hallows on the Walls are missing and the parishes of St. Edmund and St. Sidwell are not included under Exeter because they lay outside the jurisdiction of the City until 1550.[1] They would have been included in the Hundred of Wonford which encircled the city and the 1522 Survey of that Hundred does not survive.

Within the parish the names are usually divided into bowmen, billmen, aliens, those not fit to serve in a war, those living outside the parish but having lands within it and those living in the parish who presumably did not fall within the first four categories. A few women are listed, a special section in St. Kerrian's parish being reserved for ' Widows and their substance ' and the name of any servant usually follows that of the householder. In all there are 1363 entries in this survey and this must represent a large proportion of Exeter's population in 1522, the only obvious exclusions being children under sixteen years of age and the wives of householders or widowed mothers living with them. The Military Survey of 1522 is thus an extremely valuable record, not least because it includes a great many people assessed at ' nil ', for this poor element of the population was for the most part ignored by other sixteenth century tax assessments. In Exeter this portion of the population accounted for 36 per cent of Exeter's inhabitants and in Coventry, 37 per cent.[2] The number of aliens, not all poor, is surprisingly high and these included Sir Raynold Vyllayermerii, born in France, as St. George's parish priest.

The document also throws light on the pattern of land ownership in the City and the relative size of population and wealth of the parishes listed. The extent of property held by the church varied from parish to parish but was considerable. Unfortunately the ownership of property in The Close, most of it if not all owned by the Dean and Chapter, is not specified, but even excluding The Close the largest single owner of church property in Exeter was the Dean and Chapter. The church owned 60 per cent of the property in St. Martin's parish and nearly 50 per cent in St. Stephen's. Many heads of monasteries in the county had a town house in the capital city and there were also lands owned by the monastic houses like St. Nicholas Priory.[3] A considerable number of land owners were non-resident, either gentry like the Fursdons of Cadbury or descendants of old Exeter merchant families who had gone elsewhere but had retained some ancient holding in the City as had William Wylford ' of London ' in the parish of St. Martin, or William Yonge of Bristol. The City of Exeter, under the title of Mayor, Bailiffs and Commonalty of Exeter, also had a considerable holding and derived most of its income from rents at this date. A comparison of the rents of the City listed in the Survey with those given in the Receiver's Roll for 1521–2 provides the same totals for St. Petrock's parish (£5 10s) and for St. Stephen's parish (£2). The Receiver's Roll lists rents totalling £5 10s 2½d in Holy Trinity parish: the Survey's assessment of the City's

---

[1] By a charter of 8 March 1550 (E.C.A. Charter XXXV), Edward VI ratified the Act of Parliament of 2 & 3 Edward VI ' for enlarging the liberties ' of Exeter. It also stated that from that date the whole of the parish of St. Mary Steps was to be included in the City. The Manor of Exe Island, formerly a Courtenay possession and whose limits were largely co-terminous with the boundaries of St. Edmund's parish, was granted to the City of Exeter by a charter of 22 December 1550 (E.C.A. Charter XXXVI).

[2] I am indebted to Professor W. G. Hoskins for these figures.

[3] For details of the property of monastic houses in Exeter before the Reformation see J. A. Youings, ' The City of Exeter and the property of the dissolved monasteries ', *Transactions of the Devonshire Association*, 84 (1952), pp. 122–41.

rents in this parish was £5 which had been altered from £4 16s. For other parishes however the totals are widely divergent and although the sums are usually higher in the Receiver's Rolls, because the numbers involved are small no general argument could be advanced for the under-valuation of the rents and properties in the 1522 Survey. In any case the value of the City's property would be reasonably well-known and any under-valuation in the 1522 Military Survey would be obvious.

In the Exeter Survey about seven per cent of the sums given in the valuation are marked ' estimated ' and of this seven per cent, one-tenth were subsequently re-assessed. Entries altered to a higher valuation, not necessarily estimated, amounted to 102 out of the total 1363 and entries altered to a lower valuation, again not necessarily estimated, totalled only fourteen and two of these were possibly just scribal errors. This under-assessment in the first instance needs some explanation. In a few instances the householder might have been away— John Bridgeman, one of the City's M.P.'s was almost certainly in London—and the constable, a local man, in conjunction with a man's relatives or neighbours might have arrived at a sympathetic assessment. The scarcity of corn in Exeter is mentioned in Hooker's Annals in the mayoralty of John Nosworthy (Michaelmas 1521–2) and this may point to a time of general hardship,[1] but it is more probable that some men were just ' trying to get away with it '. If the re-assessments, mostly to a higher valuation, were made as a result of the instructions issued in July, it gives more exact dates for the compilation of the Exeter list. There is no evidence that the financial implications of the survey, i.e. that it was in fact a new and swingeing type of tax-assessment, were suspected by the inhabitants of Exeter.

The document

As far as is known, the 1522 Military Survey for Exeter has always been kept in the Exeter City Archives and now has the reference number Book 156a. In the 1870s the volume was noted with another by Stuart Moore when he calendared the City Archives and he designated both as ' Musters, Book 156 '. The other volume has since been found to be a list of persons paying shop fines in the city early in the reign of Henry VIII. The volumes are in a parchment cover, almost certainly of the eighteenth century, which is inscribed ' Thomas Tuppe/Ane Account Book/Receipts & Vouchers '. On the front cover is written ' Mr. Turner the Attorney, Castle Street, Exeter '. The handwriting of the volumes is similar. The Military Survey would appear to have been in the City's possession in 1544 as the names of the collectors for the 1544 subsidy, Richard Swete and Henry Maunder, are given on folio 41b. The manuscript contains 41 folios but folios 39–41 contain material not relevant to the Survey, including a list of councillors present at a meeting of the City Chamber, which was evidently never copied up. The survey has no heading but starts with the parish of St. Stephen.

THE SUBSIDY OF 1524/5

In April 1523 Parliament met at Blackfriars and Wolsey demanded a subsidy of 4s in the pound on lands and goods to be spread over four years and estimated

---

[1] E.C.A., Book 51, Hooker's Commonplace Book, fo. 338, *sub* 1521–2. Hooker makes no mention of the Military Survey being made. Harvests were bad in 1519, 1520 and 1521 (W. G. Hoskins, ' Harvest Fluctuations and English Economic History 1480–1619 ' in W. E. Minchinton (ed.), *Essays in Agrarian History*, i, p. 100).

to yield £800,000 for the prosecution of the war. The Commons remembered the recent ' loan ' and successfully protested. Among the protesters was John Bridgeman, one of the Members of Parliament for the City. John Hooker, writing later in the sixteenth century, relates [1]

'. . . In this parlament there was demaunded a subsidie of iiij^s[4s] the pounde whereat the moste parte of th[e] lower or common house grudged and murmured and no man spake more ernestly and effectually agaynst the same than this Bridgeman: w[hic]h thinges benge made knowen unto the Cardynall he sent for hym and verie sharpelye rebuked hym for it: but he meaneteaned his sayinges & at his next comnyng to the lower howse when the saide bill was agayne redd he spake agaynst it: but he had lytle thanckes for his labor and beinge in ageyn most sharpely rebuked that he never enioyed hym selff but returned to his lodginge where he fell sicke & dyed . . .'

The Subsidy Act which was finally passed granted a subsidy spread over four years. [2] In each of the first two, the tax was to be paid at the following rates: 1s in the pound on annual income from land, 1s in the pound on the capital value of goods worth £20 and upwards, 6d in the pound on goods worth from £1 to £2 and also by persons aged 16 and upwards in receipt of £1 per annum in wages. In the third year a further shilling in the pound was payable on goods worth £50 and upwards. There were additional refinements for the wealthy; those assessed at £40 or over were to pay an ' Anticipation ' a year in advance. [3] Aliens paid double rates, or if possessed of neither goods nor wages, a poll tax of 8d. Peers were to be taxed separately, [4] as were the clergy in convocation. The clergy were however assessed in the general returns for personal property which did not form part of their benefice. Goods included coin, plate and debts owed to the assessed person and allowance was to be made for the debts owed by him. The assessment excluded standing corn and personal attire.

An analysis of the distribution of wealth in Exeter as reflected in the tax assessments of 1524/5 has been made by Professor MacCaffrey and discussions of the import of the documents for Exeter's history have already been published. [5] The assessments above £40 are thought to be purely notional but those at a lower figure may represent a fair indication of a man's wealth. It has been shown that Exeter's wealth was concentrated in the hands of a few, an ' upper class ' containing 6 per cent of the population, but that the large majority of the inhabitants were to be found at the very lowest point and grinding poverty was the lot of more than half the population. A detailed

[1] E.C.A., Book 51, fo. 339, *sub* 1522–3. Bridgeman's Will dated 1 April 1523 was proved 1 March 1523/4 by his widow and relict, Alice (P.C.C. 17 Bodefeld). In April 1523 Bridgeman described himself as ' of good healthe of body '.
[2] *Statutes of the Realm*, III, pp. 230–41 (14–15 Henry VIII, c. 16). The provisions of this Act are ably summarised in Julian Cornwall, *Lay Subsidy Rolls 1524–5*, Sussex Record Society, 1956.
[3] Lists of those paying the ' Anticipation ' in Exeter survive in the Public Record Office, E.179/97/186 and E.179/96/144. These sums were due to be paid in November 1523. In February 1523/4, however, the Commissioners in Exeter were ordered by the King to send in new returns of this subsidy by Easter, as the subsidy had not been properly collected (E.C.A., Letter 3).
[4] Helen Miller, ' Subsidy Assessments of the Peerage in the Sixteenth Century ', *Bulletin of the Institute of Historical Research*, XXVIII (1955), pp. 15–34.
[5] Wallace T. MacCaffrey, *Exeter 1540–1640: the growth of an English County Town*, Harvard U.P., 1958, pp. 247–51; W. G. Hoskins, ' English Provincial Towns in the early Sixteenth Century ', *Transactions of the Royal Historical Society*, 5th series, vol. 6 (1956), pp. 1–19.

comparison of the returns for 1524/5 with those of the Military Survey of 1522 has not been made. The latter seems to point to a smaller proportion of poor people but fortunes changed rapidly in the sixteenth century. Nor is it possible to attempt to check the 1524/5 assessments of inhabitants with other records to discover if they represented a true estimation of their wealth. Practically no probate inventories of Exeter merchants survive before the 1560s, when the series of Orphan's Court inventories begin, as the wills and inventories formerly in the Exeter Probate Registry were destroyed by enemy action in 1942. Approximately one-quarter of these for the sixteenth century survive in abstract form but there is not a sufficient number surviving in these abstracts or in the Prerogative Court of Canterbury wills for any conclusions to be drawn as to the wealth of Exeter's citizens or to discover the relationship of wealth in goods or lands held by any one person. The assessment in 1524/5 was based on either lands or goods, whichever was the greater, but not both. In Exeter, however, as in Totnes and Dartmouth,[1] the men assessed at the highest amounts were those who held civic office: the prerequisite of entrance to the Council was commercial success.

Professor MacCaffrey notes a total of 956 assessments in the Exeter subsidy of 1524/5, including some illegible entries.[2] His table deals with the sums paid only and not with the names of inhabitants. The list printed in the present volume supplies just over 800 names from thirteen Exeter parishes in the 1524 subsidy and from the parishes of St. George, St. David, St. Mary Major and Holy Trinity in the 1525 subsidy, the latter parishes being defective in the 1524 list. A comparison of the lists for 1524 and 1525 where both are legible reflects the mobility of population. Names may appear in one record but not in the other. There are various reasons for this, death being the most obvious, but it is evident that there was a large floating population, probably composed of workers who frequently changed their employment. Fortunes also fluctuated, for a downward trend in some of the assessments is visible in the second year. A right of appeal was given and the appeals against the Exeter 1524 Subsidy are endorsed on the document. Unfortunately, the record is so faded at this point that few are fully legible. An abstract of those which are more or less legible appears in Appendix I. Some appeals are based on ' desperate ' debts, i.e., those that there was no hope of collecting, but Thomas Whyte of Holy Trinity claims an allowance of 15s because he has since built a house, and William Hurst, one of the richest merchants in Exeter claims against losses due to commercial disasters. The widow of John Bridgeman (see *supra*, p. xiii) claims an allowance of seven marks as she has spent £95 on the burying of her husband and the payment of his debts.

The document

The assessments of 1524/5 give two sets of figures, representing the assessed value of the lands, goods or wages and the actual amount to be levied. No local copies of these subsidies survive and the transcripts in this volume have been made from the Exchequer copies in the Public Record Office, references E.179/96/147 and E.179/96/155. Unfortunately, both are badly faded and eaten away in places.

---

[1] Laura M. Nicholls, ' The Lay Subsidy of 1523: the reliability of the Subsidy Rolls as illustrated by Totnes and Dartmouth ', *University of Birmingham Historical Journal*, IX, no. 2 (1964).

[2] MacCaffrey, *op. cit.*, p. 248.

THE SUBSIDY OF 1544

In 1543 another large subsidy was granted to Henry VIII for the prosecution of his French Wars (there had been subsidies granted at intervals in the 1530s). This too was raised in two instalments, the first in 1543 and the second (printed in this volume) in November 1544. Although the basis of assessment was similar to that in 1524/5, fewer Exeter taxpayers were listed, 786 against 809 in the list made twenty years earlier, but not a great difference overall. There are no assessments on wages in the 1544 subsidy and the number assessed on lands is higher. This may reflect rising prices and the fact that land was appreciating in value to a greater extent than goods, but a fair proportion of those assessed on lands are women, which may simply indicate that they had no ' tools of the trade ' to be taken into account when the assessment was made. Although there were minor differences between the 1544 subsidy list and the one twenty years earlier, there is no evidence in the 1544 list of the effect of the Reformation as far as the lands of the monastic houses were concerned. The purchase from the Crown of the spoils of the suppression of these houses (which took place between 1536 and 1539) was delayed until the late 1540s and even into the reign of Elizabeth and beyond.[1] The number of aliens of sufficient wealth to be included in the list is slightly higher in 1544 but there is no evidence to support the complaint voiced in 1540 regarding '. . . the infinite number of Strangers and Aliens of foreign Countries and Nations, which daily do increase and multiply within his Grace's Realm and Dominions, in excessive numbers, to the great Detriment, Hindrance, Loss and Impoverishment of his Grace's natural true Lieges and Subjects of this his Realm, and to the great Decay of the Same '.[2] Bretons and Dutchmen seem to form the largest colonies in Exeter but there were a few Scots and a gentleman with the remarkable name of Balthasar Delalow also appears in the list. John Stranger is described simply as ' alien '. Incidentally, the terms alien, denizen or inhabitant (*indigenus*) have been reproduced as written as the collectors could have drawn a distinction between the newly-arrived foreigner from overseas and the denizen. The prevalence of pinners or pinmakers in Tudor Exeter is also of interest, as this occupation was certainly fairly common in the City in the eighteenth century.

The document

No local copy of this subsidy survives and the transcript has been made from a photocopy of the Exchequer copy in the Public Record Office, reference E.179/98/247. The roll is in good condition and gives the same two columns of figures as the 1524/5 subsidy lists.

THE FOUR LATER SUBSIDIES

The subsidies of 1557/8, 1577, 1586 and 1593/5 reflect the failure of the governments of Philip and Mary and Elizabeth to rope into the tax-net as many people as those who had paid towards the subsidies of Henry VIII. During the reigns of Edward VI and Mary the governing body of powerful men had ' adjusted ' the subsidy system in their favour. It has been estimated

---

[1] J. A. Youings, *op. cit.*, p. 141.
[2] *Statutes at Large*, i, pp. 848–50, ' An Act concerning Strangers ', 32 Henry VIII, cap XVI. For ' An Act touching Strangers, what they may do as concerning apprentices, journeymen . . .' see *loc. cit.*, p. 718 (21 Henry VIII, cap. XVI).

that the Earl of Bedford (Russell), the greatest receiver of monastic spoils in Devon, had been assessed at over £1600 in 1545. In 1559, despite increased wealth, he was assessed at only £900. It was said by a Commissioner of taxes in the 1590s that the true wealth of this class was no less than twenty to thirty times greater than that expressed in the subsidies.[1]

The subsidy of 1557/8 realised over £350 from 277 taxpayers, however. Ostensibly a ' tenth ', the more usual sums paid are one-fifth on assessments on lands and approximately one-seventh on goods. Aliens having goods paid at a higher rate of approximately one-quarter and those without goods at a flat rate of 8d. By this date, however, the assessments of particular men have become notional and it is probable that the people assessed usually represent only a small proportion of the total number of households in any given parish. Yet the numbers listed in the tax assessments rose towards the end of the century, as may be seen from the following table.

Parochial Subscriptions to Exeter Subsidies 1557–1595

The number of persons paying the subsidy in each parish is followed by the total sum raised from them, given to the nearest £1.

Exeter parishes	*1557–8*		*1577*		*1586*		*1593–5* (Sums paid not given)
All Hallows Goldsmith Street	22	£24	10	£4	13	£3	14
All Hallows on the Walls	4	£1	3	under £1	4	£1	9
Holy Trinity	10	£9	16	—	20	£5	23
St. David	9	£7	9	£2	20	£3	18
St. Edmund	10	£8	9	£2	10	£2	12
St. George	16	£9	21	£5	12	£2	19
St. John	8	£10	14	£6	13	£5	16
St. Kerrian	13	(?)£8	14	£4	16	£4	19
St. Lawrence	13	£12	12	£4	17	£5	11
St. Martin	23	£33	27	£12	27	£13	33
St. Mary Arches	21	£39	17	£7	19	£7	19
St. Mary Major	37	£42	46	—	36	£9	49
St. Mary Steps	10	£7	10	£2	14	£2	14
St. Olave	16	£29	17	[over £5]	21	£8	18
St. Pancras	7	£8	8	£3	9	£2	11
St. Paul	4	£8	6	£1	10	£2	11
St. Petrock	23	£70	33	£18	36	£15	42
St. Sidwell	18	£10	18	£3	28	£4	24
St. Stephen	13	£22	6	£2	13	£5	11
TOTAL	277	£356	296	£94*	338	£97*	373

* denotes sum given in document, not necessarily the total of this column.

The figures also reflect the shift of population thought to be worth taxing from one part of the city to another, for instance to the parishes of St. Petrock, St. Mary Major and St. George within the walls and to the parish of St. David outside the walls, the latter showing the increasing popularity of a house in the

[1] A contemporary view was that of Francis Bacon: ' The Englishman is most master of his own valuation and the least bitten of any purse in Europe '. I owe this reference and the figures concerning the Earl of Bedford to Professor W. G. Hoskins.

suburbs as the merchant made his money, although it was not until the late seventeenth century that the City's estate at Duryard was developed to any extent.[1]

The documents

The assessment of 1557/8, which survives in the Exeter City Archives, is not dated and the space preceding the assessment normally filled in by an indenture appointing collectors is blank. The names of ' John Peter mayre ' and two others appear at the head of the document. Peter was mayor of Exeter in 1557/8, 1562/3 and 1575/6[2] but the assessment printed here can be ascribed to his first term of office for the following reasons: firstly, the subsidy levied in his second term is dated and survives in the Exeter City Archives and secondly, a comparison of the burials recorded in the surviving Exeter parish registers establishes that several men whose names appear on the list had died shortly after 1557/8. The document has four membranes, some stained, and is generally rather dirty. The remains of some of the seals are still attached.

The assessment made on 14 September 1577 has four exceedingly fragile membranes and that of the second payment of a subsidy granted in Parliament on 29 March 27 Elizabeth I (1585) and dated 5 September 1586 has three.[3] Both of these give two columns of figures as in the 1524/5, 1544 and 1557/8 assessments.

The last item printed in this volume is in a slightly different format and gives only the assessment and not the sum which was to be paid. It is a file of nineteen papers containing assessments for the various Exeter parishes and each paper is signed by at least four of the commissioners. The names of the taxers or collectors are also given in most parishes. One paper, for St. Martin's parish, is noted as relating to the first payment of the last subsidy granted in the Parliament of 35 Elizabeth I (1593). Five others bear various dates in September 1595. With the exception of the Cathedral Close, all Exeter parishes are covered, although the lists for St. Edmund (p.10 of the file) and St. George (p.3 of the file) are not described as such.

The later subsidies, therefore, are disappointingly thin for the genealogist and not until 1641 and 1660 are the lists of taxpayers more comprehensive.[4] Also the later sixteenth century lists seem to have been rather carelessly written for to quote but one example the William Perie in St. George's parish in the 1586 list was very probably the same person as the William Pavie who appeared in the 1593/5 subsidy. A list during Elizabeth's reign comparable in its scope with the Military Survey of 1522 would have been of immense value. For the late sixteenth century more sources of another kind survive, however. Two-thirds of Exeter's parish registers are extant from the end of the century and there is a fragmentary parish rate for the parish of All Hallows Goldsmith

---

[1] J. A. Youings, *Early Tudor Exeter: the Founders of the County of the City*, University of Exeter, 1974, p. 27.

[2] M. M. Rowe and J. Cochlin (eds.), *Mayors of Exeter from the thirteenth century to the present day,* Exeter City Library, 1964.

[3] This document was formerly numbered Miscellaneous Roll 76 in the Historical Manuscripts Commission's *Report on the Records of the City of Exeter* [Cd. 7640], 1916, p. 402. It has since been placed with other local copies of tax assessments, all of which have the reference E.C.A., pressmark Z6.

[4] See W. G. Hoskins (ed.), *Exeter in the Seventeenth Century: tax assessments 1602–1699*, Devon and Cornwall Record Society, new series 2, 1957.

Street.[1] A recent discovery was a list of inhabitants of the parish of St. Mary Major who subscribed to the Queen's lottery in 1568[2] and this is particularly useful in that it lists several, if not all, members of a number of households in the parish.

A comment on the 1524/5 subsidy rolls for Sussex was that they concealed as much as they exposed[3] and this is true to a greater or lesser extent of all the documents printed in this volume. Nevertheless, where the information contained in them is taken in conjunction with other sources, some already in print,[4] they cannot be neglected by any historian of Tudor Exeter.

Editing Practice

All entries have been translated into English except where the document was defective and the phrase was obviously unfinished. Christian names (except for the names of some aliens), occupations and place-names have been modernised as far as possible. If the modern form is in doubt, the original has been italicised and appears in round brackets following the modern form i.e. Cleves (*the land of Clyve*). Where no modern form exists the name has been italicised. In the Military Survey of 1522 the spelling of the military equipment listed and the headings under which the parishioners are normally divided, such as bowmen, aliens, etc., have been standardised. Throughout, editorial notes interpolated in the text have been placed in square brackets and three dots indicate that the document is defective. Arabic numerals are used except where the amount is obviously incomplete. No attempt has been made to supply the second figure, i.e. the tax payable, by deduction from the valuation of goods, wages, etc., or to correct any apparent discrepancy between the two sets of figures in the assessments for 1524/5, 1544, 1557/8, 1577 and 1586, or to correct the deficiencies of Tudor accountancy, for it is sometimes difficult to see how a particular sum was estimated, especially in the 1524/5 subsidy. The headings of the 1489, 1524, 1544, 1577 and 1586 subsidies have been abstracted in modern spelling, but retain all the relevant details. In Appendix I the appeals against assessment in the 1524 subsidy have been abstracted also, where they were legible. A full transcript of these appeals was not feasible because of the poor state of the document, nor was it possible to trace in the text all the persons so appealing, as the 1524 assessment itself was defective.

ACKNOWLEDGEMENTS

I should like to thank Professor W. G. Hoskins and Professor Joyce Youings for their help and encouragement with this volume. The publication of these particular assessments was Professor Hoskins' idea and he kindly lent me the photocopies of the 1524/5 and 1544 subsidies so that the work could be done almost exclusively in Exeter. I am indebted to Professor Youings for her

---

[1] East Devon Record Office, All Hallows Goldsmith Street Parish records, PX 2.

[2] *Ibid.*, St. Mary Major Parish Records, PW 1. See M. M. Rowe and T. J. Falla, ' The Queen's Lottery 1568 ', *Devon and Cornwall Notes and Queries*, XXXIII, pp. 240–3.

[3] Julian Cornwall, *Lay Subsidy Rolls 1524–5*, Sussex Record Society, 1956, p. xxxiii.

[4] *The Description of the Citie of Excester by John Vowell alias Hoker*, transcribed and edited by Walter J. Harte, J. W. Schopp and H. Tapley-Soper, Devon and Cornwall Record Society, 1919 and 1947; Rowe and Jackson, *Exeter Freemen*.

invaluable advice on both the content and the presentation of the volume. The Exeter City and Devon County Councils have kindly given their permission for the documents in the Exeter City Archives to be published and the Controller of H.M. Stationery Office has permitted the publication of Crown copyright documents in the Public Record Office. The staff of the East Devon Record Office rendered valuable assistance with the index and finally I should like to thank them and the County Archivist, Mr. P. A. Kennedy, for their forbearance in listening to the many problems of Tudor taxation.

Exeter, 1976.   MARGERY M. ROWE

THE TENTH OF 1489

[Abstract of Heading] Indenture made 7 March 4 Henry VII [1489] between Richard Druell, Thomas Calwodeley and Henry Hanneford, commissioners of the King of the one part and John Sterre, John Bokyngham, Nicholas Hamelyn, William Baker, Walter Yorke, John Wylkens, Richard Cleff, John Mirevild, John Walssh, Henry Redeway, Hugh Page and John Lake, named as collectors for the city of Exeter and its suburbs by the commissioners for the levying and collecting of the tenth part of the annual value of issues and profits of all lands and tenements and of goods and chattels to the value of 10 marks or more, as appears in an Act of Parliament dated 13 January last past.

Richard Wagott, William Whitelok', Richard Germyn, Walter Champeons, John Burgeis, Stephen Claw, Philip Attwyll, Stephen Mattecote, John Leche, Robert West, John Clyfton and William Pyle bear witness to this.

[m.1] Executors of Thomas Hayley by Martin Noris	16d	The same Johane by John Lewys	2s
Robert Hyll by John Walssh	3s	John Bonefaunt by William Robyns and William Spicer	8s
Thomas Calwodeley by Agnes Grene	10d	Leonard Giffard by Matilda Hyll	21d
Wardens of the Church of St. Lawrence by John Hunkyn	12d	The same Leonard by Margaret Fyssh	21d
John Cowham by William Fayreman	10d	The same Leonard by William Pyke	2s 8d
John Chambernon by John Tregis	2s 8d	The same Leonard by Isabella Paxe	18d
John More by Roger Shordych	2s 8d	The same Leonard by Peter Harewode, John Danaster and Giles Vendersale	8d
Richard Wagott by John Natyre	3s		
Robert Hill by Petrock Smyth	2s 2s	Richard Germyn for 4 tenements	3s 2d
John Odyll by John White, barber	16d	John Harris for himself	16d
Robert Hill by Thomas Erle	21d	John Colshull by Giles Vendersale	4s
Earl of Devon by William Naynow	20d	The same John by John Harris	2s 8d
Thomas Calwodeley by Simon Carreu	2s 4d	Richard Germyn for himself	7s 2d
The same Thomas for himself	2s 8d	John Seyntcler' by Thomas Coterell	2s 8d
The same Thomas by William Cannell	2s 4d	John Crockehay by John Rowter	23d
		Richard Germyn for himself	9d
The same Thomas by Giles Adam	19d	Richard Clyffe for himself	2d
Johane Richemond by Anthony Pynnow, Matthew Rogger and John Wateis	2s 1d	John Pollard by Nicholas a Burne	9d
		John Browne by Ralph Nerbert	6d
		John Sterre for himself	8d
The same Johane by Hugh Lawson	12d	Thomas Dogmanton for himself	6d
The same Johane by John Bereman	9d	Matthew Jubb by John Snell	12d
Thomas Olyver for himself	6s	Richard Turner by John Auger	2s 8d
John John by John Nicholl	2s	Thomas Fulford, knt., by William Oset	16d
The same John by Thomas Nicholl	19d	John Crocker, knt., by Giles Vendersale	5s 4d
Johane Richemond by John Lampray	2s		
The same Johane by John Soper	19d	Matthew Alynton for himself	8d
The same Johane by Nicholas Hattemaker	19d	William Obley by John Hoper	2s 8d
		Nicholas Prous by Nicholas Wever	9d
The same Johane by John Segour	3s 6d	Leonard Giffard by John Kayleway	16d
The same Johane by Henry Netherton	8s 3d	Thomas Style for himself	2s 8d
		John Stukeley by Anthony Pefort	2s 8d
The same Johane by Peter Harewode	3s 3d	William Pascow by Henry Lowryng	2s 6d
The same Johane by Richard Clyff	19d	Simon Davy for himself	3d
The same Johane by Anthony Pynnow	19d	John Fowacres by Richard Renewyll	2s

John Sayer by Anthony Iswyn	3s 6d	The same John by John Wylkyns	2s
John Batyn by Stephen Clew	3s	Mr John Attewyll for himself	5s 4d
John Heyngston by Peter Cholmore		Johane late the wife of John Oryng	4s
and Richard Renewyll	2s 4d	Johane Richemond by William	
Thomas Fulford, knt.	9d	Bynkys	6s 8d
[m.2] John Calwodeley for himself	4s	The same Johane by Robert Brow	16d
Heirs of Robert Wylfford by Robert		The same Johane by John Parker	5s 2d
Chubb	2s	Nicholas Nawn & Robert Code by	
John Hyndeston by John Wyll,		Elizabeth Raley	8s
baker	21d	The heirs of John Oryng by Matthew	
William Courtenay, knt., for himself	4s	Alynton	8d
Matthew Jubb by Walter Kever	10s 8d	Robert Chubb by Richard Fyssh	10d
Thomas Bounde for himself	4s	The same Robert by John Michell	10d
Thomas Style by John Slugge	7s 4d	The same Robert by John Coryer	6d
John Chalvedon by Elizabeth Treffrie	9s 2d	The same Robert by Reginald Gumby	10d
Henry Hull, esq., by Robert Chubb	8s 2d	The same Robert by John Gumby	10d
The same Henry by John Colshull	10s 4d	The same Robert by Robert Bonefaunt	19d
John Wagott for himself	4s	Margery Bowdon by Robert Bonefaunt	21d
John Sidnam by John Hooker	10s 2d	Matilda Bonefaunt for herself	12d
John Waddam, knt., by John Thomas	19d	Thomas Penhale for himself	4d
The same John by John Wylkenson	2s 2d	Richard Savery for himself	8d
The same John and Nicholas Blewett		Thomas Flexhale by John Gotor	9d
by Robert Newton	16d	Matthew Alynton for himself	2s
The same by John Stanbrigge	2s 1d	John Symon, clerk, by John Walssh	6s 8d
Thomas Crymell for himself	12d	The same John Symon by John	
Heirs of Robert Wylfford by Henry		Whiddon	2s
Stevyn and Robert Brenden	3s	John Bere by John Mattecote	2s 7d
Thomas Burneby by John Fursse	2s	John Germyn by William Page	2s 4d
Rector of the Church of St. Kerrian		Thomas Bowryng by [blank]	19d
by Nicholas Hattemaker	12d	The same Thomas by William Trote	4d
John Betty by William Naynow	4s	Matthew Jubb by Robert Bokeram	2s 3d
The same by John Tylham	2s 8d	The same Matthew by James Tyott	23d
The same John by Thomas Parker	10d	The Earl of Devon by Stephen	
The same John by William Groce	10d	Mattecote	8d
John Lang by Michael Swetebody	12d	Richard Germyn by William	
John Tayler by John Mewy	16d	Byllynges, John Pers & Stephen	
Thomas Saris for himself	12s 8d	Mattecote	23d
John Bevys for himself	20d	Christine Fenecote by John Gerveis	3s 8d
Robert Newton for himself	8d	William Hyll by Levi Yeo & John	
Peter Wyllyam by Richard Row	2s 8d	Hill, shearman	3s 3d
Robert Newton by John Burgeis	4d	William Larder by John Bryddel-	
Peter Wyllyam by Thomas Foxe	2s 8d	lyngton	12d
The same Peter by Thomas Lagharne	14d	Nicholas Prous by John Blynne	9d
The same Peter for himself	8d	John Bere by Reginald Bowhaye	8d
John Betty by John Lang	4s	Johane Ruggemond by John White	11d
The heirs of Robert Gambon by		The same Johane by Henry Faux,	
Richard Yoldon	4s	Humphrey Hauke & Roger Dyssh	5d
The said heirs by John Tregasew	12d	Thomas Pyke by Margery Abraham	16d
The heirs of John Pollard by Thomas		[m.3] The same Thomas by Thomas	
Coteler	19d	Kerver	6d
John Harris by Hans Marshall	19d	Nicholas Hamelyn & Roger Dyssh	2s 4d
John Colle by William Blome	2s 2d	Henry Hull	14d
Ivan Pafford by Martin Benett	4s 8d	John Wadham by John Bere	8d
John Sidnam by John Betyn	8s	John Chalvedon	19d
James Harris for himself	3s 2d	John Wisewold	12d
Henry Hull by Thomas Snow	16d	Thomas Mewy for himself	7d
The same Henry by Thomas Provest	16d	Henry Hull by John Mattecote	2s
Raymund Kyrton by Thomas Marke	2s	Ralph Bokelond	12d
John Symon for himself	4s 8d	John Clyfton for himself	19d
John Bonefaunt for himself	5s 4d	William Cosyn by Thomas Bertelett	22d
John Gumby for himself	2s	Elizabeth Treffrey by William Tope	15d
John Batyn by Elizabeth Werthe	6s 8d	Peter Row for himself	21d

Robert Russell	4s
Richard Renewyll	4s
John More by John Blamie	2s
The heirs of Walter Bampfeld	2d
Richard Clerk by John Beer	3s
Leonard Gifford by John Wateis	3s 4d
John Browghton by Matthew Rogger	3s 2d
Lewis Pollard by John Philypp	19d
Leonard Gyfford by John Coke	8d
The same Leonard by Thomas Burnard	8d
The same Leonard by William Shilston	10d
John Simon, clerk, for 4 messuages	5s 4d
Leonard Giffard by John Cote	20d
William Whetelok by Richard Lake	4d
Henry Hull by Anthony Raynes	3s 4d
Walter Champeons for himself	4s
Margaret Mathew for herself	5s 4d
Thomas Calwodeley by John Weston	3s 2d
The heirs of Robert Wyllefford by Robert Crues	2s 8d
The same heirs by Richard Cleffe	2s
The same heirs by Geoffrey Lewis	2s 8d
The same heirs by William Osett	6s
Elizabeth Treffrey by Richard Pavy	4s
John Pollard by Henry Webber	2s
John Sterr for himself	2s
Robert Hoker for 3 tenements	6s
John Sidnam by John Bokyngham	5s 4d
The same John by Robert Hoker	5s 10d
The heirs of Richard Wolston & John Germyn de pynner	7s 4d
Peter Wyllyam by Henry Hanneford	4s . . .
Henry Hull by John Parker	5s 4d
William Geter for himself	3s 4d
James Chuddeley by Brian Kykeley	2s
Richard Helyer by Richard Stykes	4s
Master William Elyott, clerk, for himself	16d
James Chudley, esq., for himself	8d
The same James by John Thomas	2s
Elizabeth Bernard for herself	15d
William Oru by Reginald Forsterster [sic]	4s
The same William by John Paynter	16d
The same William by John Budde	19d
William Stoner, knt.	4d
Thomas Calwodeley by John Doke	16d
The same Thomas by Reginald Forster	16d
Henry Hull by Simon Pays	10d
The same Henry by William Pocok	7d
The same Henry by Margaret Tapster	8d
John Bykyngton by John Raley	4s 4d
John Herte for himself	2s
Nicholas Blewett, esq., by John Berden	8d
John Sydnam by Robert Hall	12d
Matthew Jubbe by William Peter	2s
The executors of John Palmer	16d
John Sayer by Peter Markett	12d
Richard Crokhay by William Peter	16d
John Atwyll by Walter Slader	11d
Walter Champeons	11d
Walter Yorke by [Walter Yorke deleted]	3s 4d
The same Walter by John Pers	2s 8d
The same Walter by John Lake	2s
The same Walter by John Hervy	8d
The same Walter by Richard Duke	19d
The same Walter by Agnes Acland	7d
The same Walter by Henry Pytte	7d
John Berdon for himself	8d
John Bonewyle by John Hoigge	6s 8d
John Attwyll by Simon Blake	2s
The same Philip [sic] by John Brymsdon	6d
The same Philip [sic] by John Brabon	6d
The same Philip [sic] by William Sporer	16d
William Bowden by Richard Druell	3d
[m.4] William Malerbe by John Leche	4s
Leonard Gyffard by John Buktofte	18d
Richard Druell for himself	9s 4d
John Sapcote, knt., by Richard Druell	20d
George Chepman by Henry More and others	22d
John Hoker by Peter Gregory	19d
The same John by John Stoddon	2s 8d
The same John by Emmotte Turner	22d
The same John by Mr. John Charlis	8d
The same John by John Gybbis	6s 4d
The same John by John Gerveis	19d
The same John by Henry Thryng	16d
The same John by [blank]	9d
The same John for 6 other tenements	3s 2d
John Shappecote, knt., by Robert Russell	5s 5d
Gilbert Yerd by John Reever	2s
William Baker for himself	4s 8d
Richard Hurle for himself	12d
John Camell for 4 tenements	2s 1d
Hugh Cause by John Lanard	6d
. . . de la Pomeraye by John Stoddon	9d
. . . Frenssh by Thomas Pederton	16d
. . . Cornelis	9d
. . . tro Broke for himself	3s
. . . he Sayer	16d
Richard Withebroke	17d
Richard Sangwyn	3s 2d
Elizabeth Werth for 1 stable	16d
Philip Atwyll for himself	5s 4d
Thomas Calwodeley by John Wall	16d
Robert Lydoll by John Bence	2s
William Obley by Elizabeth Cornyssh	21d
The same William by John Tokerman	8d
. . . Clerke by John Wynnecote	6s 4d
. . . re Hyndeston by Thomas Dampsell	19d
. . . Hull by Thomas [blank]	2s
. . . Colyn by Henry Clerke	11d
The same for one other tenement there	4d
Robert Russell by John Brian	6s

Richard Skelton by John Skelton	3s
Richard Helyer by John Wyse	19d
The same Richard for himself	4s
The same Richard by Nicholas Sawndy	12d
The same Richard by Lambert [sic]	21d
Walter Courtenay, knt.	9s 4d
William Frenssh	3s
Hugh Cause by John Cosyn	4s 8d
William Drew by Thomas Cruys	6s 8d
. . . Hamelyn by Richard Northern	6s 8d
. . .beth Werth by John Dolle	2s 8d
. . .to Batyn by William Cleyhanger	3s 4d
. . . Holond by Giles Colchett	2s 4d
. . . Obley for himself	2s 8d
The same William for other tenements	11s
. . . Levermore by Giles Colchet	2s
Thomas Calwodeley by John Coll	4s
Matthew Goldsmyth	11d
John Down	13d
The same John for himself	12d
Wilmot Fursdon by John Bense	2s 8d
William Lang for himself	3s
Richard German by Richard Vyncent	2s
William Burnard by Richard Poleman	9d
The same William by William Smert	8d
. . . Poleman for himself	15d
. . . Ruggewaye by John Ruggewaye	2s 8d
. . .rt Chubb for 2 tenements	4d
. . . Ruggewaye by John Ruggewaye	2s 4d
. . . Pyke by John Pawlyn	4s
. . . Bowdon by John Claissh	2s 8d
. . .a Calwodeley by Hugh Artor	18d
. . .	2s
. . .orke for 3 tenements	21d
. . . Wadham & Nicholas Blewet	9d
[He]nrico Redeway by John de Vale	2s
John Grygge for himself	2d
William Farewyll by Richard Bertelet	2s
Margaret Coterell	2s
John Fursdon by William Lampray	3½d
The Earl of Devon by William Montegu, clerk	3s
John Orynge for 3 tenements	6s 6d
The same John for 2 tenements	19d
Ralph Bokelond for 3 tenements	3s 10d
John Wadham, knt., by Henry Faux	4d
Thomas Benett by Gilbert Waryn	2s
John Weston for 3 tenements	4s 10d
John Ruggeway by Humphrey Hauke	19d
Henry Faux for 2 tenements	8d
Nicholas Hamelyn & Stephen Ruggewaye	9d
John Bowdon by John Taylour	7d
John John by Pendynges	8¼d
Stephen Ruggewaye for himself	6s
Elizabeth Trefrie by Nicholas Hamelyn	4s
John Wadham, knt.	6s 4d
[m.5] Richard Batyn by Christine Fenecote	5s 5d
William Trote for himself	4s
John Devyok by Richard Savery	2d
The same John by Richard Dixton	18d
Elizabeth Trefrey	2s 1d
Matthew Chubbe by Thomas Perkyn	2s 4d
William Trote by Nicholas Hegge	16d
Martin Ferrers by Henry Moliche	10s 4d
The same Martin by Henry Wanneford	12d
Elizabeth Trefrey by Nicholas Coley	. . .d
John Stapilhill by John Colchet	13d
Wardens of St. Martin by Stephen Mattecote	22d
The same Wardens by Thomas Alyn	30d
Thomas Langworthy for himself	5s 4d
Roger Holond by John Ectour	5s 4d
The same Roger by John Gervys	6s . . .
The same Roger for one cellar	. . .
The same for one tenement	. . .
Margery Bowdon	. . .
The same Margery	2s . . .
Roger Holand	4d
The Earl of Devon	. . .
John Pollard	. . .
James B . . .	
The heirs of William . . .	
James Curs . . .	
John Wad . . .	
Thomas . . .	
Henry . . .	
. . . skynner	. . .
. . .	
. . .itys	10s . . .
. . .	. . .d
. . . John Gybon . . .	2d
. . .	12d
. . .erte	9d
Richard Renewyll	6d
John Hoker	8d
John Sterre	6d
John Atwyll by John Slader	2d
John Hamont by John White	22d
William Whiteloke by Edward Smyth	12d
The Wardens of St. David	6d
John Colle by Richard Blewett	16d
William Naynow for himself	8d
Peter Wyllyam for himself	19d
John Wadham, knt., [and] Nicholas Blewett by Thomas Dampsell	8d
The Wardens of St. Petrock by Richard Bury	12d
Peter Wyllyam	16d
John Wadham, knt. by Richard Levermore	2s 8d
Henry Hull by Roger Brounscomb	2s 8d
John Wadham, knt. & Nicholas Blewett, esq. by John Mattecote	2s 8d
Henry Hull by John Ruggewaye	14d
Ralph Hill by John Sayer	8d
Henry Horne	18d
John Averye	16d
Stephen Frend	10d
John Betyn	19d

John Wadham, knt. [and] Nicholas		Ri . . . Helyer	. . . 6d
Blewett, esq. by John Parker	2s 8d	John Sterre . . .	2s
The same for Burymede	2s 2d	Nicholas Prous	12d
Henry Redeway	5d	Thomas Calwodeley	22d
Hugh Stucley by Robert Rendell	12d	Thomas Estmont	. . . 6d
The heirs of John Kelly by William		William Legh . . .	
Otis	2s 8d	John Sidenham . . .	
Thomas Coteler	6d	William Wylfford . . .	
John Sym for himself	6d	[m.6] Richard Sterre . . .	
John Getor	6d	Roger Shordyche . . .	
Thomas Style by William Dobyn	7d	John Risby . . .	
John Harris by Thomas Parker	8d	John Newcomb, clerk, . . .	
William Cosyn	9d	Thomas Eveleg . . .	
Henry Skynner	8d	John Somayster . . .	
John Betyn	12d	John Halwyll . . .	
Matthew Jubb by John Ruggeway	4s	William Whitelok	6d
Henry Hull by John Colshull	4s	Christopher Cressha	6d
John Wadham, knt. [and] Nicholas		Christopher Crochay	. . .d
Blewett, esq. by John Betyn	2s	John Harry	13 . . .
The same by Nicholas Whetecomb	13d	Margery Page . . .	
Henry Hanneford	12d	William Obley . . .	
Stephen Mattecote	12d	John Colle . . .	
John Danaster	8d	Johane Pedeler . . .	
John Bustard by John Coll	22d	Richard Wagott . . .	
John Sidnam by Agnes Glyngham	2s 8d	John Colsshull . . .	
Henry Redeway	2s 8d	Thomas Levermore . . .	
Robert Hill	3s 1d	John Symon . . .	
John Weston for himself	4d	Philip Vicary . . .	
William Knyght	2s	Robert Eton . . .	
John Wadham, knt. [and] Nicholas		Robert Leyman . . .	
Blewett, esq. by John Lang	5s 8d	John Wadham et . . .	
Thomas Fulford . . .		[Remainder illegible and incomplete]	
Ralph Hyll	7s . . .		

THE MILITARY SURVEY OF 1522

PARISH OF ST STEPHEN
Constables, viz. Richard Duke, Hugh Payge and John Holmer
The store of the said parish church amounts to nil

Bowmen able for the war
William Peryman, a bow, a half sheaf of arrows and a sallet, in goods, 20s
John Carter, servant to William Pery, a bow and half sheaf of arrows, 20s
William Huchyn, a bow and half sheaf of arrows, 40s
John Holmer, harness for a man, 20 marks

Billmen able for the war
John Mutton, a sword and buckler, 20s
Peter Sprynge, a bill, a sallet and a pair of splints, 14s
John Crowdycotte, a bill, 6s 8d
John Potter, a bow and a sword, 10s
Richard Drake, apprentice to John Bodlegh, nil
William Warde, servant to Robert Trowe, nil

Aliens . . . *for the warre bylmen*
Mighell Pepyn, born in Normandy, harness . . .
Cornely Carver, a Dutchman . . . ESTIMATED
Barberd Johnson, Dutchman . . .

Not able for the war
Roger White, harness for a bowman, in goods, £10 [£6 deleted]
Roger Bolter in goods, £100 [£20 deleted]
Richard Duke, harness [*for a man* deleted] for 2 billmen, 100s [*marks* deleted]
[f.1b] Richard Scoos and Richard Duke, servants of the said Richard Duke, nil
Thomas Balard in goods, 40s
William Lange, servant to William Peryman, nil
Thomas Hawkyns, servant to Peter Sprynge, nil
Henry Lener and Edmund Myddelton, apprentices to Peter Sprynge, nil
Richard Coke, fletcher, a bow, a sheaf of arrows and a pair of brigandines, £6 13s 4d
   [£4 deleted]
Richard Webber and John Townesen, servants and apprentices to Richard Coke, nil
Thomas Richard, labourer, nil
Richard Glovier, nil
Hugh Page, a bow and arrows and harness for a man complete, 100 marks
Ralph Denson, servant of John Crowdycott, nil
Richard Harte, complete harness for a bowman, £10 [5 *marks* deleted]
Randulph Revell, servant to the said Richard Harte, nil
Robert Bysshopp, servant [*sic*] of Richard Harte, nil
Geoffrey Holmore, servant to John Holmore, in goods, nil
John White, capper, in goods, 13s 4d [*nil* deleted]
Th . . . hanyng, harness for 2 billmen, £30
. . . per, 40s [10 *marks* deleted]
. . ., nil
. . . Coc . . . harness for 2 men complete, £30
Nicholas Roter, harness for a man, £10 [£5 deleted]
Robert Trowe, harness for a man, 20 marks
Robert Grene, servant to Robert Trow, nil
John Grenewode, servant to Robert Trow, nil
[f.2a] James Rodys, harness for 2 men, £6
John Maunsell, carpenter, nil ESTIMATED

7

Aliens
William Coloff, Dutchman, a bill, a sallet and a pair of splints, 13s 4d
William Browne, servant to William Coloff, nil
Peter Cosyn, 20s
Farmelowe, servant to *myladies grace*, born in Picardy, 40s ESTIMATED
Thomas Wayse, clerk, parson of the parish, whose benefice is worth per annum, £12
Robert Hygges, curate, in goods, 5 marks
Thomas Lebene, nil

Those which live outside the parish but have lands within
The Abbot of Hartland, per annum, 28s 8d
The Dean and Chapter of the Cathedral of St Peter of Exeter, £13 4s
Roger Arundell, esq., £4 2s 8d
Robert Turner and Elizabeth his wife, £3 2s 8d
William Ratclyff, 20s
Thomas Fuller, 46s 8d
The Mayor, Bailiffs and Commonalty of the City of Exeter, 40s
Giles Hyll, esq., 46s
The Prior of the House of St John the Baptist of the same City, 36s 8d
The Abbot of the House of Newenham, 10s
[f.2b] John Noseworthy and Henry Atwyll, per annum, 48s 8d
The Vicars of the Cathedral of St Peter of Exeter, 8s
The Prior and Convent of the Friars Preachers of the said City, 26s 8d
The heirs of Richard Clerke, 20s
The Wardens of the goods and chattels of the parish of St Mary Major [*our lady the more*] of the
    City of Exeter, 20d
The *Chauntor* and College of the Church of the Holy Cross of Crediton, 40s
John Thomas Courtholder and Thomas Gyfford, 20s
The heirs of Stapylhyll, 8d
Gilbert Kyrkeby, 40s

[f.3a]   PARISH OF ST MARTIN
Constables viz. William Mathew, William Davy and John Holmer the elder
The store of the said parish church amounts to £6

Bowmen able for the war
Richard Seynthyll, servant to Doctor Caselegh, harness for a man, £4
[*Stephen Smyth in goods* deleted, 20s ESTIMATED
Thomas Wescott, servant to Stephen Lorymer, nil
Nicholas Lymett, harness for a man, £50
John Holmer the elder, harness for a man, £20

Billmen able for the war
Thomas Bevys, servant to the City, harness for a man & worth in goods, £6
William Mathewe, harness for a man & worth in goods, 10 marks
Richard Foke, a sword and buckler, servant to Doctor Talet, 30s
The same William has in tenements per annum, 36s

Those not able for the war
Geoffrey Lewys, harness for 2 men, 40 marks
Nicholas [blank], servant to the same Geoffrey, nil
John Scoos, harness for a man, £60
The same John has in tenements per annum, £4
Thomas Bassett, a sallet, a bill, and worth in goods, 10 marks
Thomas Taverner, harness for a man, £20 [*marks* deleted] ESTIMATED
Thomas Monday, a bow and a sheaf of arrows, nil
Gilbert Waren [*Martyn Coffyn* deleted], a pair of brigandines, a sallet, a bill and is worth ir
    goods, 10 marks
William Davy, harness for a man, and is worth in goods, 60s
[f.3b] William Peke, harness for a man, and is worth £20
Ralph Raddon, servant to Thomas Bevys, nil

Henry Cutberde, a bill and is worth 6s 8d
Robert Slogge, a harness for a man, and is worth nil ESTIMATED
John Hals, a bill, and is worth nil
John Bryndon, a sallet and a bill, and is worth 13s 4d ESTIMATED
Richard Atkynson, a bill and is worth 13s 4d
John a Grauntham, a pair of splints, a bill and is worth 13s 4d
John Jonson is worth 20s
Stephen Lorymer, harness for a man and is worth £7 [100s deleted]
Thomas George, a breastplate and a bill and is worth 20s
Edward Hyllersdon, harness for a man and is worth 30s ESTIMATED
Henry Mocke, harness for a man and is worth 100s ESTIMATED
Nicholas Betton, a bill, a sallet and is worth 6s 8d ESTIMATED
Thomas Courtes, a bill, a sallet and is worth 30s
Johane Beaumont, widow, is worth 60s ESTIMATED
Margery Panter, widow, is worth 20s ESTIMATED
William Torre, parson of the said parish, in goods, £12
The profits of the same benefice are worth per annum, £10
Gilbert Carter, chantry priest, 20s.
Thomas Shyrwyll, chaplain, is worth 40s
Roger Shirman, clerk, is worth £10 ESTIMATED
Petrock White is worth 20s
Richard Paschow, chaplain, is worth 40s

[f.4a] Aliens
Martin Queffyn, born in Normandy, a sallet, a bill and is worth 20 marks
John Bokebender, born in Normandy, servant to the said Martin, is worth 10s
Peter Calff, born in Holland, is worth 20s
John Hatmaker, born in Brabant *abyllman for the warr*, has harness for a man and is worth 40s

Those which have lands within the parish but live outside
The Dean and Chapter of the Cathedral Church of St Peter, £22 12s
William Yonge of Bristol, £4 6s 8d
The Prior and Convent of the House of St John the Baptist of the said City, £10 4s 8d
William Sares of Kent, 13s 4d
William Wylford of London, £8 18s 4d
Prioress and Convent of St Katherine of Polsloe, 16s
The Prior and Convent of the House and Church of Plympton, 57s 4d
John Calwodlegh, esq., 32s 4d
William Radclyff, 46s 8d
Hospital of St Mary Magdalene, 4s
The Mayor, Bailiffs and Commonalty of the City, £4 16s
John Hulle, 26s 8d
Vicars of the Cathedral Church of St Peter of Exon, £11 12s 4d
Johane Hawkyns of Taunton, widow, 40s
Thomas Gefford, 20s
Thomas Goodman, 16s

[f.4b]   PARISH OF ST PANCRAS
Constables viz. William Hurste, William Cotyner and William Totyll
The store of the said parish church amounts to £4

Bowman able for the war
John Hopkyn, harness for a man and is worth in goods, 100s

Billmen able for the war
John Parr worth in goods, 20s
William Burscotte, a bill, a pair of almain rivets, a sallet and is worth in goods, 40s
John Jones, a sallet, 2 bills and is worth in goods, 26s 8d
John Stephyn, a bow and is worth in goods, nil

Those not able for the war
Thomas Benbowe, parson of this parish, whose benefice is worth 106s 8d

The same Thomas has in goods £20
William Aysche, priest, is worth in goods 53s 4d
William Cotyner, harness for a man and is worth in goods £26 13s 4d [£20 deleted]
The same William in lands by the year 40s
Giles Lamberd servant to William Cotyner, nil
Richard Rythe, apprentice, nil
Johane Bonde, widow, lands by the year 26s 8d and is worth in goods £9 ESTIMATED
Geoffrey Parre, harness for a man and is worth in goods 20 marks [£10 deleted]
John Thomas, fisher, harness for a man and is worth 40 marks [£23 6s 8d deleted]
William Totyll, a sallet, a bill, a field of mail and is worth £10 [10 marks deleted]
[f.5a] George Horton, harness for a man and is worth in goods £4
[John Kever is worth in goods nil deleted] ESTIMATED
John Seller is worth in goods £10
[blank] Bonde, widow [in a later hand].
Johane Metrygaver alias Polglas, widow, is worth in goods 20s ESTIMATED
[Richard Ratclyff is worth in goods £10, in a later hand]

Those which have lands within the parish but live outside
Thomas Parson per annum 20s
John Bury of Colyton, esq., 32s 4d
The Hospital of St Mary Magdalene 10s
William Chenals 26s 8d
The Mayor, Bailiffs and Commonalty of the City aforesaid 19s 4d
The Prior and Convent of Plympton 7s
The Prioress of the House of Polsloe £3 16s 8d
The Dean and Chapter of the Church of St Peter in Exeter 100s
The Vicars of the same Church 33s 4d
The Prior of St Nicholas of the said City 16s
William Courtney, knt. £3
Peter Eggecomb, knt. 8s 4d
The heirs of Wynard to the use of the almshouse 31s 8d
The feoffees of John Baron for to send leghte of St Pancras Church 6s 8d
Charles Faryngdon, gent. 20s
John Wadham, gent. 20s
John Hulle 3s 4d
John Beere of Huntsham 10s

[f.5b]   PARISH OF ALL HALLOWS GOLDSMITH STREET
Constables Thomas Olyver, John Garmyn and John Yoe [Holmer deleted]
The store of the said parish church amounts to 56s

Bowmen able for the war
Walter Jamys is worth in goods 40s
John Morelegh, servant to John Carter, is worth in goods nil
William Deyman is worth in goods nil
Hugh Warde is worth in goods 40s [nil and 20s both deleted]
William Bade, fletcher, is worth nil

Billmen able for the war
Robert Dyrham is worth in goods 10s
Nicholas Abell, a Dutchman born in Bruges (Byrges), a breastplate and a knife and is worth 10s
John Hamount is worth in goods nil
John Teylle, born in Holland, is worth in goods nil
Thomas Gryge, harness for 2 men and is worth in goods £10
John Northbroke, complete harness for a bowman and is worth £10 [10 marks deleted]
Roger Marche, a sallet and a bill and is worth £3 [20s deleted]
Anthony Water, born in Cleves (the lond of Clyff) and is worth nil

Those not able for the war
John Germyn, a pair of brigandines, a sallet, 2 bills, a pole axe and is worth 40 marks
The same John has tenements per annum worth £4 0s 8d

Andrew Mannyng, a pair of splints, a bow, 2 sheaves of arrows, a bill, a fall of mail, a pair of
    gussets and is worth 20 marks [£10 deleted]
John *Trehar* is worth in goods 26s 8d
Richard White is worth in goods nil
John Totyn, goldsmith, a Frenchman born in Rouen (*Rone*) and is worth 40s
John Sholder, born in Cleves (*the land of Clyve*), harness for a man, £40 [£30 deleted]
[f.6a] Thomas Edwardes is worth in goods nil
Richard Lardes is worth in goods nil
John Inglysche, born in Lombardy, is worth in goods nil
Henry Nottelles, a Dutchman, is worth in goods nil
John Carlyon, servant to Nicholas Abell, is worth nil
John Carter, harness for a man and is worth £10 ESTIMATED
John Nuton, servant to John Carter is worth nil
Cornelius Morys, a Dutchman, servant to the same John Carter is worth nil
Thomas Corsett, a halberd and is worth 20s
Stephen Peter is worth in goods 20s
James Hatmaker, born in Lucca (*lond of Luke*), is worth 13s 4d
Robert Robelett, born in Normandy, is worth 10s
John Vylffayne, harness for 2 men and is worth £20 [*marks* deleted]
The same John per annum 26s 8d
John Drue, servant to the same John is worth nil
Peter Masyn, servant to the said John is worth nil
John Dyer is worth in goods nil ESTIMATED
John Lane, a pole axe and is worth £20 [*marks* deleted]
Robert Peter is worth in goods 40s [20s deleted]
John Yoe, harness for a man and is worth £120 [£110 deleted]
John Richard, 3 bills and is worth £4
Waryn Edward, servant to John Richard, 20s
Robert Fermer, a bow, a half sheaf of arrows and is worth £6 [£60 deleted]
William Stephyn, harness for a man and is worth 20 marks ESTIMATED
Nicholas Stokker, servant to Sir William Courtney, knt., is worth nil ESTIMATED
Thomas Wyllys is worth in goods nil
[f.6b] Thomas Olyver, harness for a man and is worth in goods £10
The same Thomas has per annum 43s
John Nicholl, harness for a man and is worth £30
The same John has per annum 13s 4d
Andrew Brygan is worth in goods 10s
John Golde is worth in goods nil
Roger Bysell, a Dutchman, is worth in goods nil
Sir John Tregethew, parson of this parish is worth in goods £20 and his benefice is worth by the
    year £10

Those which have lands within the parish but live outside
William Colswyll of London £4 8s 8d
Thomas Gyfford per annum £6
John Bonyfaunt £4 13s 4d
John Huytte per annum 23s 4d
John Bery per annum £6 9s
The Dean and Chapter of the City of Exeter 34s 8d
The Prior and Convent of St John of Exeter 26s 8d
Sir Richard Sydner 51s
Robert Bery 29s
Henry Hamlyn 52s

[f.7a]   PARISH OF ST KERRIAN
Constables Robert Buller and John Sydenham
The store of the parish church amounts to 18s
Thomas Benbowe parson for his benefice per annum £6 13s 4d

Bowmen able for the war
William Burges, harness for himself and is worth in goods £6

John Martyn, servant to William Burges, is worth nil
Lancelot Harnys, servant to doctor Talett, is worth £6 ESTIMATED

Billmen able for the war
George Aylesbere, servant to John Crugge is worth nil ESTIMATED
William Bucker', a bill and is worth in goods nil
David Blake is worth in goods £10
John Taillour, servant to John Crugge is worth nil ESTIMATED
Thomas Grygge, harness for a man and is worth £10

Those not able for the war
John Burges, a bill, a standard of mail, a pair of gussets, a fall of mail and is worth £5 ESTIMATED
John Crugge, harness for 2 men and is worth in goods 400 marks ESTIMATED
The same John in lands and tenements by the year £5
Thomas Bremylcomb is worth in goods £3
Henry att Wyll, servant to my lady grace, is worth in goods nil
John Venycomb, servant to Robert Brygman is worth 40s [33s 4d deleted]
John Harrys, harness for 2 men and is worth £10
John Sydenham, harness for a man and is worth £10 [£5 deleted]
Humphrey Androwe, harness for a man and is worth £100
Christopher Myxstowe, a bill and is worth 20 marks [£10 deleted]
Thomas Fynemore nil
[f.7b] Alexander More is worth nil ESTIMATED
John Spenser, a jack, a pole axe and is worth 4 marks [40s deleted]
William Wandrake nil ESTIMATED
John Rowlond nil
Robert Brygman is worth in goods £3 [40s deleted]
Geoffrey Jerston is worth in goods 20s
John Wayll, a bill, a sallet and is worth nil
Richard Downe is worth 40s
Robert Juke is worth in goods [*harness for himself* written above]
William Hayn, servant to Bremelcomb is worth nil
John Lynan nil

Those which have lands within the parish but live outside
Thomas Benbowe, parson, per annum 9s
John Wadham of Carderston 5s
William Baron of London 53s 4d
The Vicars of the Cathedral Church of St Peter in Exeter £3 6s 8d
John Scose 16s 8d
John Wakelyne 30s
Juliana Vygors, widow, 16s
Thomas Hexte 40s
Walter Pollard of Plymouth 15s
The Prior of St James of the said City £4 20d
Agnes Froste, widow, 26s 8d
Richard Androw 26s 8d
The Wardens of the Church of St Martin 6s 8d
[blank] Estmond of the county of Somerset 12s
Master Sydnor *Chanon* 26s 8d
[f.8a] The Wardens of the Church of St Kerrian 6s 8d
Humphrey Collys and Hugh Colles 26s 8d
[blank] Pafford of North Tawton 20s
Johane Sydenham, widow, of Culmstock, 18s 2d
John Thomas and John Waggytt 4s
The Prior of Plympton 6s 6d

Widows and their substance
Anna Crugge, *votissa*, is worth in goods 400 marks ESTIMATED
Alsyn Bente, widow, £20

[f.8b]   PARISH OF ST PAUL
Constables William Peke, Richard Chubb and John Tuckefeld
The store of the said parish church amounts to 20s

Bowmen able for the war
Robert Toker, harness for a man and is worth in goods £10
Walter Hoper, servant to Edward William is worth nil
Richard Brownemede, a bow, a half sheaf of arrows and is worth 10s
Robert Wescott, a bow, a half sheaf of arrows and is worth 20s
John Forde, a bow, a half sheaf of arrows, and is worth 20s
John Prynce, a bill and is worth 20s
Edmund Grebyll, a bow, a half sheaf of arrows and is worth 10s
John Harrys is worth in goods nil
Richard Hoppkyns is worth in goods nil

Billmen able for the war
Peter Schere, born in Holland, a bill and is worth 40s
Hugh Pope, servant to the same Peter, is worth 20s
Garett Grownyng, born in Friesland, a bill and harness and is worth nil
Thomas Trebyll, a bill and is worth nil
Robert Cundett is worth in goods 10s
William John is worth in goods nil

Those not able for the war
Johane Hull, widow, is worth in goods £10 [£6 deleted] ESTIMATED
The same Johane has in tenements per annum 20s
John Awellys, harness for a man and is worth in goods £30 [£20 deleted]
William Coper, servant to Robert Toker is worth nil
[f.9a] John Bartlett, carrier, a bill and is worth in goods 20 marks [£10 deleted]
Matthew Moyfyld, servant to John Bartlett, and is worth nil
Thomas Farewell, a jack, a sallet, a bill and is worth 4 marks [40s deleted]
Edward Williams, a sallet, a bill and is worth 40s
John Elys, servant to Edward Williams, and is worth 8s
Thomas Heth, harness for a man and is worth £3 [40s deleted]
William Keyward, servant to Thomas Heth, is worth nil
Richard Taillor, a bow, a half sheaf of arrows and is worth 20s
Richard Lorymer, a bow, a half sheaf of arrows and is worth £10 [10 marks deleted]
John Richard, servant to Richard Lorymer, is worth nil
Nicholas Baker, a bill, 20s
John Hewys, a bill and is worth 20s
Thomas Pawle, a bill and is worth 20s
William Davy, a sallet, a bill and is worth 20s
William Lesewyll, tailor, a bill, 20s ESTIMATED
John Cheryton, a bill and is worth 6s 8d [nil deleted]
Richard Barewell is worth nil
Thomas Markys, a bill and is worth nil
John Trotte is worth nil ESTIMATED
Richard Rotynbery is worth nil ESTIMATED
William Ogyer is worth in goods nil ESTIMATED
Richard Hylle, a bill and is worth nil
John Swayn, hellier, is worth nil
Henry Locke, servant to Robert Wescott, nil
[f.9b] Simon Edwards is worth in goods nil
William Skynner is worth in goods nil
John Tuckfylde, brewer, harness for a man and is worth in goods 20 marks [£8 deleted]
Thomas Gagge, servant to J Tuckfeld, is worth in goods nil
James Selond, a Fleming, servant to John Tuckfeld, nil
Richard Chubbe, harness for a man and is worth £20
John Olyver, servant to Richard Chubbe and is worth 20s
William Penycott, servant to the same Richard, and is worth nil
Robert Cosyn, servant to the same Richard, is worth nil
John Browne is worth 13s 4d

John Cannyng is worth nil
John Byschoppe, parson, is worth in goods 40 marks and his benefice is worth by the year £10

Those that have lands within the parish
Certain men that are seised of lands to the use of this church for certain obits to be had and
    said yearly 13s 4d
The Abbot of Buckland has yearly rent 26s 8d
The Abbot of Torre has per annum 14s
The Prior of St John of the aforesaid City £6 7s 2d [14s deleted]
The Prior of St Nicholas of the aforesaid City 6s 8d [32s 9d deleted]
The Prior of Pilton 3s 4d
The Prioress of Polsloe 20s
Elizabeth Pomerey 32s
Sir Richard Paschowe 20s
Lord Fitzwaren 21s 4d
Thomas Stuckley of Afton 13s 4d [20s deleted]
[f.10a] Nicholas Kyrkham £4
Anthony Pollard 6s
Walter Pollard of Plymouth 9s 6d
John Trebylyon 4s
Humphrey Walron of Bradley 8s
John Beare of Huntsham 14s 8d
John Eistmunde 9s
John Germyn 10s
John Smyth of Bridgwater 12s
Clement Crokhay 12s
William Radclyff 50s
John Hylle of *Agenswylle* 12s
Alice Dente, widow, 20s
The Feoffees and Wardens of St Mary Major (*Seynt Mary the more*) 2s 4d
Thomas Gyfford 7s
John Thomas Courtholder 20s
Nicholas Langmede 20s
John Barre of St Giles 12d
Thomas Marlowe, 10s
William Hurste 10s
William Gylberd 4s
Roger Yorke 18s
Thomas Bonyfaunte 7s 8d
John Goldsmyth 7s 8d
William Brygges 7s 8d
John Bonyfant the elder 20s
[f.10b] The Brethren of the Cordwainers (*Brotherredyn of the Cordeners*) of the said City 13s 4d
William Husy 8s
Robert Davy, tailor, 7s
John Hynxe 7s
The Dean and Chapter of St Peter of Exeter 3s 4d
The Mayor and Commonalty of the City of Exeter 3s 4d
The Wardens of Exebridge 2s
The Feoffees of Wynard's almshouse £3 13s 4d

[f.11a]   PARISH OF ST MARY MAJOR
Constables William Benett, Robert Hoker and William Sommester
The store of the said parish church amounts to £4

Bowmen able for the war
John Cheryton, harness for himself and is worth in goods 20 marks [£4 6s 8d deleted]
Benet Glubbe, servant to the city, and is worth in goods 20s ESTIMATED
Henry Karans, servant to Sir William Carew, knt., is worth in goods 20s
Richard Barbour is worth in goods 13s 4d
Thomas Isacke, harness for himself except half a sheaf of arrows and is worth in goods 20s

John Smyth, a sallet, and is worth 10 marks [60s deleted]
William Glanfeld, a bow and is worth nil
Geoffrey Barbur, a bill, harness for himself, a bow, and is worth £8 [£6 deleted] ESTIMATED
John Keyth, servant to Sir William Courtney, knt., harness for a man and is worth 10 marks
    [40s deleted]
John Fynne is worth nil
John Briggeman, harness for 2 men and is worth in goods 40 marks ESTIMATED
Henry Clerke is worth 20s
Thomas Stephyns, harness for himself, is worth 10 marks [40s deleted]
John Philyppe is worth nil
Nicholas Baker is worth nil
John Fursdon, a bow, a sheaf of arrows and is worth 26s 8d
John Dyxton, a bow, a sheaf of arrows and is worth nil
William Lowe, servant to John Keth, is worth nil

[f.11b] Billmen able for the war
John Garett, harness for a man and is worth £20
William Bebery is worth 20s
Richard Bassett is worth harness for himself, £20
William Motlycote, servant to Sir Thomas Wise, clerk and is worth[1] 20s ESTIMATED
William Worseley, servant to the Bishop of Exeter, is worth 100s ESTIMATED
John Trenchard is worth 40s
William Howell, harness for a man and is worth £40
John Jonys is worth in goods nil
[John Martyn, servant to Mr. Alnot Arscotte, clerk, is worth 20 marks, deleted]
Nicholas Plummer, servant to William Courtney, knt., is worth 100s
John Cleyhanger is worth £6
Thomas Beauforest, servant to Sir William Courney (sic), knt., is worth £8 [100s deleted]
Richard Polyng is worth nil
John Noppy, harness for a man and is worth £6
John Golde is worth 10 marks
John Damsell, harness for 2 men and is worth £20
John Herewode is worth 20s
Thomas Sanbury, servant to Robert Hoker, nil
Simon Frende, servant to Walter Howyll at Corner and is worth nil
[Hugh Hyggys, harness and is worth (blank) entered in a later hand]

[f.12a] Those not able for the war
John Alyn is worth in goods £10 [100s deleted]
Juliana Vygours, widow, harness for a man and is worth £10 [£20 deleted] ESTIMATED
John Porter, a jack, a pair of splints, a bill and is worth 40s
William Coblonde is worth nil
Christopher Partrigge, harness for a man and is worth 10 marks ESTIMATED
Walter Rondell, harness for a man and is worth £30
John Davy is worth in goods 40s
John Wayt is worth 13s 4d
William Albryght, a breastplate, a bill, 20s
John Humfray, harness for a man and is worth 20s
James Shomaker, born in Holland, is worth nil
Walter Howyll at Corner, harness for a man and is worth 10 marks
Thomas Ligher, a bill and is worth 20s
William Benett, harness for 2 men and is worth 40 marks
John Ryppley is worth 20 marks ESTIMATED
John Wolcotte the elder is worth 100 marks
John Wolcott the younger is worth £10 ESTIMATED
John Balam, harness for 2 men and is worth 100s
William Hyllynges, a bow, a sheaf of arrows and is worth 20s
Richard Russell, harness for 2 men and is worth £40 [£10 deleted]
Vitall Forde, servant to Sir Nicholas Hensthow, is worth nil
William Somaster, harness for 2 men and is worth £20
Robert Hoker, harness for 2 men and is worth £40 ESTIMATED

Entry crossed through and non hic quia in parochia sancti Laurentii written above.

John Englond, a sallet and is worth in goods 10s
[*John Walle, goldsmith, is worth* 40s in a later hand]
[f.12b] Edward Deylond, harness for a man and is worth in goods £40 [£6 deleted]
Walter Trotte, a bow, a sheaf of arrows and is worth £7
Thomas Cottyner, harness for a man and is worth £10 [*marks* deleted]
John Whytfylde, harness for a man and is worth 20 marks
John Polleslonde is worth £10
William Schere is worth nil
John Bonyfant, harness for a man and is worth 20 marks [£4 deleted]
Robert Norway is worth 20 marks
Richard Hoper is worth nil
Richard Avery is worth 40s [15s deleted]
Thomas Cookes is worth in goods 20s
Roger Edley, harness for a man and is worth nil
John Martyn, servant to Alnot Arscote, clerk, is worth £20 [*marks* deleted]
Robert Alway is worth nil
Richard Palmer is worth 40s
Walter Bagtor is worth nil ESTIMATED
Stephen Ketyll is worth nil
John Byrde is worth nil
Richard James is worth nil
Richard Dyxston, harness for a man and is worth 20 marks [£6 deleted]
William Lotte, harness for a man and is worth 10 marks
Garet Schomaker, born in *Duchelond* and is worth 6s 8d
John Papyngay, born in France, is worth nil
Richard Martyn is worth 6s 8d
Henry Wellys is worth 6s 8d
Richard Call, a bow, a sheaf of arrows and is worth nil
[f.13a] Richard Row is worth 10s

Aliens
Cleofas Capper, a Frenchman, is worth 53s 4d
Gyllam Skynner, a Breton, is worth nil
Robynet le Jaunder, a Frenchman, a billman worth 20s
Gelys Curryer, a Frenchman is worth 40s
John [blank], his servant, a Frenchman, is worth nil
John Tremont, a *briton*, is worth nil
Rawlyn Mynnett, a *briton*, is worth 4s
Ewyn Jego, a *briton*, is worth 13s 4d
Nicholas Herte, servant to Robert Norway, is worth 26s 8d
Gyllam Deme, servant to the same Robert, 20s
Adam Prydeaux, Thomas Peter [and] Philip Isacke, servants to Thomas Isacke and are worth nil
Richard Bragge [and] Thomas Corsey, servants to Walter Howell and are worth nil
Gelys at Courte, born in Flanders
John Hammondes, servant to Richard Dyxston, is worth 40s
Thomas Barne, servant to the same Richard and is worth nil
John Eggeman, servant to John Clevehanger, is worth nil
Edward Sykleng, servant to the same John, is worth 13s 4d
John Claysche, servant to William Lotte, is worth nil
William Estcotte, William Geffrey, [and] William Salle, servants to John Byrgeman and are worth in goods nil
[*Thomas Sceby, baker*, 40s entered in a later hand]
[f.13b] Benet Horne, servant to Walter Hole & Corner, is worth nil
John Stephyns, servant to John Humfray, is worth nil
Nicholas Benett [and] John Monstevyn, servants to William Dene, are worth nil
John Sarke, servant to Richard Russell, nil
Thomas Smarte, servant to John Trenshard, nil
John Wythham, servant to John Noppy, is worth nil
John Potter is worth nil
Mr. Laurence Dobell, parson of this parish, for his benefice worth by the year, £20
Sir John Bowdon, curate, is worth £10

Sir Henry Bury, priest, is worth 26s 8d
The said Mr. Laurence Dobell is worth in goods £30
Mr. Thomas Brerewode is worth £50 ESTIMATED
Sir Roger Goldsmyth nil
Sir Robert Faireman £10
Sir Stephen Cruys is worth 30s [nil deleted]
Sir Oliver Henscott nil
Sir Nicholas Dyxton, £4[1]
Sir John Porter is worth nil
John Knyght, a bill and is worth 100s [20s deleted]
John Morgan is worth nil

Those that have lands within the parish
The Prior and Convent of Plympton, £10
The Dean and Chapter of the City of Exeter, £8
The Mayor and Commonalty of the City of Exeter £5
William Vycary £4
William Catroll 6s 8d
John Tottyll 35s
John Crugge 40s
John Fortescue of Filleigh 6s 8d
Lord Fitz Waren £3 6s 8d
Robert Hoker £10
The Bishop of Exeter 100s
The Abbot and Convent of Tavistock 10 marks
John a More 40s
Maistras Chudley 26s 8d
The Prioress and Convent of Polsloe 4s
John Bere of Huntsham 10s
Mr Speke with other feoffees of Wynard's almshouse £4
The heirs of Nicholas Goseham 6s 8d
The heirs of Marwode 10s
The Vicars of the Cathedral Church of St Peter 20s
Henry, Earl of Wiltshire 30s
The Abbot and Convent of Newenham 26s 8d
My Ladys Grace of Devonshire 26s 8d
Walter Pollard 10s
Henry Colyng 6s 8d
George Gyffron 13s 4d
Thomasine Herne 13s 4d
Peter Caselegh and other feoffees of James Chudley 39s
The Prior and Convent of St Nicholas of the aforesaid city 13s 4d
f.14b] Henry Copelston 20s
John Carew 20s
Sir Nicholas Wadham 13s 4d
William Radclyff 13s 4d
Richard Polyng 30s
Mr William Gybbys 36s 8d
Mr Ayssheford 16s
The heirs of Fursdon 13s 4d
John Orenge 6s 8d
Nicholas Langmede 13s 4d
John Bury of *Colaton* 20s
The heirs of Henry Hull 16s
The heirs of William Cosyn 23s 4d
Roger Graynfeld, esq., 20s
Ralph Pudsey 10s
Henry Attwyll 20s
Mr Gerard Hel' 20s
The heirs of Thomas Andrewe 13s 4d entered in a later hand]

[1] Entry crossed through and *non hic set in parochia Sancti Georgii* written above.

[f.15a]   PARISH OF ST PETROCK
Constables John Thomas, Richard Martyn and John Ducke
The store of the said parish church amounts to 40s
Thomas Acclon, parson of the same parish, is worth £10 and his benefice per annum £26
Thomas Nyelde, servant to the parson, is worth 10s
William Herne, chaplain, is worth £11 [£8 deleted]

Bowmen able for the war
Edward Hylman, servant to John Symon, and is worth 20s
Richard Rugge, servant to Mr More, and is worth nil
John Wylcoke, servant to Nicholas Kyrkeham, and is worth nil
William Parson, servant to John Ducke, and is worth nil
Peter Streche, harness for 2 men and is worth 100 marks
Edward Scher, harness for a man and [blank] 10 marks
Thomas Wanell is worth nil
Thomas Sandyford, servant to Mr Adam Trainer, clerk, a bow, a sheaf of arrows and is worth
     nil
Richard Hunte, a sallet, 2 bills and is worth in goods £10
Robert Frere is worth in goods 20s
Nicholas Grysby, barber, is worth nil
William Gumbey is worth in goods 20s

Billmen able for the war
Ralph Rugge, servant to Mr John More and is worth nil
Peter Blackmore, *a moren borne* is worth in goods nil
William Comyng, servant to Mr John Thomas is worth nil
John Wollecott, harness for a man and is worth £10
Thomas Hele is worth 20s
Robert Bele is worth nil

Those not able for the war
John Calwodelegh, esq., harness for 4 men and is worth £30
The same John has tenements by the year 40s
John Trevareke, servant to the said John Calwodlegh, is worth nil
John Calwodley, servant to the same J Calwodlegh is worth nil
John Symon, esq., harness for 4 men and is worth 100 marks
The same John in lands by the year 46s 8d
John Wylle, servant to the same John Symon, and is worth nil
John More, gent., harness for 4 men and is worth £40
John Bawdon, servant to the same John More, nil
Nicholas Kyrkeham, esq., harness for 2 men and is worth £20 ESTIMATED
The same Nicholas in lands £7
John Heyne, servant to the same Nicholas is worth nil
Richard Martyn, gent., harness for 2 men and is worth 100 marks
John Courtney, servant to the same Richard, is worth nil
Thomas Cutten, servant to the same Richard, nil
Paul Faunte Colyn, a Dutchman, servant to the same Richard, a gunner and is worth nil
William Hurste, harness for 2 men and is worth £100
The same William in lands 20s
Thomas Swetelonde, apprentice to the same William, nil
John Philepp, apprentice to the same William, nil
John Brycknoll, harness for 2 men and is worth £200
John Vaughen, his apprentice, nil
Robert Cotten, apprentice and is worth nil
Robert Buller, harness for 2 men and is worth £200
John Buller, harness for 2 men and is worth £100 ESTIMATED
Thomas Hunte, harness for 2 men and is worth £100
John Boner, apprentice with the same nil
[f.16a] John Thomas, harness for 2 men and is worth £20
Leonard his son is worth nil

Thomas Fuller, harness for a man and is worth £10
John Lewys, apprentice, nil
John Wagott, harness for a man and is worth £8
The same John in lands 26s 8d
William Buckenam, harness for a man and is worth £24
John William, apprentice with the same William, nil
John Ducke, 2 bows, a sheaf of arrows and is worth £10
John Deyman, servant to Peter Streyche, is worth nil
Robert Trekyll, servant to the same Peter, is worth nil
John Wynter, servant to Edward Schere, is worth nil
John Burlace, a jack, a bill and is worth £10 [£8 deleted]
Robert [*John* deleted] Northebroke, harness for a man and is worth £10 [£8 deleted]
William Chanon, a bow, a half sheaf of arrows and is worth £8
William Shyldon, apprentice to the same William, nil
Richard Smyth, a bill and is worth £8 [10 *marks* deleted]
Thomas Provest, harness for a billman and is worth 10 marks
John Rasselegh, apprentice to the same Thomas, nil
William Wanell is worth 10s
Henry Bystatour, a Dutchman, is worth £3
Luke [blank] his apprentice, a Dutchman, is worth nil
John Wodebeare is worth nil
Robert Wyndeayte, servant to Robert Freer, is worth nil
Iwen Codleyn, a *Bryton*, 20s
[f.16b] Henry Burlace is worth nil
Hugh Tylleacre, pinner, is worth 20s
William Colyn, saddler, is worth nil ESTIMATED
John Purser is worth 40s ESTIMATED
John White, cook, servant to Lord Fitzwarren, 40s ESTIMATED
Richard Denys is worth £4
John Stote, apprentice to Margaret Buckenam, is worth nil
Margaret Buckenam, widow, harness for 2 men and is worth £10 ESTIMATED

Those which have lands within the parish but live outside
[blank] Syddenham, widow, £8 19s 6d
The Dean and Chapter of the Cathedral Church of St Peter in Exeter £12 8s with 40s of a
    pension issuing out of St Petrock's church
The Vicars of the same place 48s 8d
The Countess of Devon £6 6s 8d
The Abbot and Convent of the monastery of Syon 12s
The Prior and Convent of Launceston 8s
The Prior and Convent of St Nicholas of Exeter 10s
The Prior and Brethren of St John of Exeter 13s 4d
The Mayor and Commonalty of the same city £5 10s
The Wardens of Exebridge (*the Brugge of Exa*) 23s 2d
The Hospital of Mary Magdalene of the aforesaid city 12d
Thomas Merlar 33s 8d
John Bere of Huntsham (*Hunssam*) 60s
Nicholas Wadham, knt., 22s
[f.17a] The heirs of Nicholas Bluet 17s
The heirs of William Wynard £8 10s
John Bourchier, Lord Fitzwaren, 12s
John Hull 43s 4d
Robert Hoker £3 5s
Walter Pollard of Plymouth 61s
John Wadham of Caterston 20s
John Bonyfaunt £4 13s 4d
John Wolston of Staverton 13s 4d
John Calwodlegh and other feoffees of Thomas Eliot, esq., 13s 4d
William Benett and Richard Russell for the performance of a will 18s 2d
The feoffees of Robert Wyllefford for the performance of his will 35s
The Prior and Convent of Plympton 15s

[f.17b]   PARISH OF ST MARY ARCHES
Constables John Brycknoll, Richard Androw and Robert Smyth
The store of the said parish church amounts to £5
Robert Froste, parson of the same parish is worth £14 [£16 deleted]
Sir William Redway, parish priest, is worth £40
Sir William Jane, 40s

Bowmen able for the war
Hugh Davy, harness for himself and is worth £10 [marks deleted]
John Cowyke, servant to the same Hugh, is worth nil
The son of William Alyn junior is worth nil
John Tukeffyld, harness for himself and is worth £6

Billmen able for the war
William Bude, servant to Gilbert Kyrke and is worth nil
William Exbrige, servant to Hugh Davy, and is worth nil
John Herte, servant to Doctor Talett is worth 26s 8d
John Trubody is worth £20 ESTIMATED
John Kedelton, goldsmith, is worth 40s

Those not able for the war
Mr John Bradmorè, harness for 2 men and is worth 400 marks
The same John has lands, £4 8s
Richard Tanner and John Carter, his apprentices, are worth nil
William Forest, harness for 2 men and is worth 100 marks ESTIMATED
Thomas Hamton, his servant, is worth nil
Wimond Austyn, harness for 2 men and is worth £16 ESTIMATED
Richard Swette, his servant, is worth 10s
The same Wimond has lands 8s
[f.18a] Christopher Lamberd, harness for a man and is worth 100 marks
John Hassard, his apprentice, is worth nil
John Amore, harness for a man and is worth £40 ESTIMATED
John Blakaller, harness for 2 men and is worth 100 marks ESTIMATED
Richard Androw, harness for 2 men and is worth £80
The same Richard has in tenements per annum 18s
Thomas Browne, his apprentice, is worth nil
Gilbert Kyrke, harness for 2 men and is worth 200 marks
The same in tenements per annum £8
Geoffrey Wylston, William Gyfford and John Growte, his apprentices, are worth nil
Mistress Anys Froste is worth £60 ESTIMATED
Item in lands 53s 4d
Richard Faux, harness for a man and is worth 100 marks
Robert Smyth, harness for a man and is worth £30
John Way, harness for a man and is worth 100 marks
The same John in annual rents 20s
Richard Mylle is worth in [blank] £5
Robert Groger, his servant, £5
William Brugge, harness for a man and is worth 33s 4d
Richard Lymeber', his servant, is worth 33s 4d
Thomas Bonyfaunt is worth £10 ESTIMATED
William Massy is worth 100s ESTIMATED
William Alyne the elder is worth in goods 100s [£4 deleted]
Awen Cheney and Andrew Yeben, servants of John Tuckfeld, are worth nil
John Burnyng, skinner, is worth 40s
Thomas Grene, his apprentice, is worth nil
Thomas Hassard is worth 20s ESTIMATED
Elspeth Rowlond, widow, is worth 20s ESTIMATED
Richard Mawdett, servant to John Carow, is worth nil
Elspeth Luschant, widow, harness for a man and is worth 100s [40s deleted] ESTIMATED
The same Elspeth in tenements 41s 8d
[f.18b] Richard Dowell is worth nil
Matthew Langworthy is worth nil

Davy Niell is worth 10s
Johane Holmer, widow, is worth 10s ESTIMATED
Johane Saffre, widow, is worth 10s ESTIMATED
William Blowdon, servant to Richard Faux, is worth nil
The parish clerk, called John Stevyns, is worth nil

Those which have lands within the parish but live outside
John Carew of Antony £3 6s 8d
Walter Courtney £4 2s
My lady of Polsloe 25s
William Fursdon of Cadbury 33s 4d
John Fursdon of Tiverton 25s 8d
The Vicars of the Cathedral Church of St Peter in Exeter £3 3s 4d
Thomas Beire, baker, 20s
The Prior of Launceston 16s 8d
Henry Hamlyn 23s 4d
Nicholas Langmede 19s 8d
John Paynter junior of Plymouth 14s
Henry Atwyll £10 16s 10d
The Prior of Plympton 6s 8d
The Dean and Chapter of the Cathedral Church of St Peter 13s 4d
Richard Fursdon 13s 4d
John Fursdon of Cadbury 13s 4d
[f.19a] The Prior and Convent of St Nicholas of the City of Exeter 11s
Robert Landon 12s
The heirs of Bluet 8d
Sir Thomas Denys, knt., and other feoffees of the will of Thomas Androw £3 18s
The Mayor and Bailiffs of the aforesaid city 50s 4d
John Bradmore and Wimond Austyn, feoffees of certain land 33s 6d

[f.19b]   PARISH OF ST OLAVE
Constables Henry Hamlyn, William Peryham and Roger Luxton
The store of the said church amounts to 2s 4½d
Thomas Banyster, parson of this parish is worth 100s ESTIMATED
Item his benefice per annum £8
Sir John Brukcha, curate is worth in goods 40s

Bowmen able for the war
Roger Luxton, harness for 2 men and is worth £100
John Trobrygge, servant to Doctor Michell, a bow and half a sheaf of arrows, 40s
John Huchyn, a bow and is worth 40s
William Underhay, a bow, a sheaf of arrows and is worth £3
Richard Wolston is worth in goods 10s

Billmen able for the war
William Dreton, a pair of brigandines, a sallet, a pair of gussets, a standard and is worth £10
Thomas Rede, 2 halberds, a pole axe and is worth £10 [*marks* deleted] ESTIMATED
George Ayere, servant to Thomas Harres, nil
Laurence Prowse, harness for a man and is worth nil
The same Laurence has by the year 26s 8d
John Smyth is worth nil

Those not able for the war
John Lewys, Prior of St Nicholas, 2 bills and a pole axe and is worth 100 marks
The same Prior has lands by the year £4 9s 4d
Robert Robyns, John Toker and John Mussell, servants to the Prior, are worth nil
William Cassella, servant to the Prior, is worth 20s
William Wyxsted, a bow and a sword and is worth nil
[f.20a] John Kente, a bow, a half sheaf of arrows and is worth 40s
Henry Colton, a bow, a half sheaf of arrows and is worth £20
Robert Hyll, a bow, harness for a man except a sallet and is worth 40s

William Hasard, a bow, a half sheaf of arrows and is worth nil ESTIMATED
Richard Ratclyff, servant to Doctor Michell, a bow, a sheaf of arrows and is worth 100s
John Rademan, a bow and is worth nil
Henry Hamlyn, harness for 2 men and is worth £100
The same Henry has in lands 40s
Robert Batyn and Nicholas Hamlyn, his servants, are worth nil
William Peryham, harness for himself, 2 bills, a sallet, a pair of splints, a gorget and is worth
  £200
The same William has in lands 48s
Roger Webber, his servant, is worth nil
Thomas Hogge, harness for 2 men and is worth £100
The same Thomas in lands by the year 40s
John Peramore, his servant, is worth 20s
John Cradocke, a halberd, a forest bill and is worth £6
William Geldon, a bill and is worth 20s
Thomas Harrys, harness for a man, a pair of brigandines, a sallet, a bill and is worth £200
  ESTIMATED
The same Thomas has in lands 40s
Thomas Wybber is worth nil
John Symons is worth 10s ESTIMATED
James Tyatt, a bill and is worth 20s
William Rede is worth 10s
Robert Come nil
Thomas Hawke 10s
Richard Bere is worth 20s
[f.20b] William More for Drayton his servant is worth nil
Underhay the servant of William Holmys, is worth nil
Robert Cotoner, a bill, a pair of splints and is worth £7
John Whyddon, 2 bills and is worth £10 [marks deleted]
The same John in lands 20s 8d [28d deleted]
John Hamont is worth nil
David Richard is worth nil
Walter Whyddon, servant to J Whiddon, is worth nil
John Merygrene is worth nil
William Burton, servant to John Huchyns is worth nil
Margaret Weston, 2 pairs of brigandines, 2 bills and is worth £10 ESTIMATED
Stephen Denys, a Frenchman, is worth nil
John Lothe, *a bryton*, is worth nil

Those which have lands in the parish but live outside
The feoffees to the use of the will of Thomas Androw, £3 6s 8d
Richard Ferys 40s
John Fransys and William Schapton 32s
Thomas Beire, baker, 20s
The Wardens of the parish of St Martin 53s 8d
Hugh Younge of Bristol 10s
John Bere of the South Hams 32s
John Symon £4
Thomas Stapulhyll 10s
John Lymscotte 10s 4d
The Prior of the House of St John of the same City 13s 4d
The Prior of Plympton 6s 8d
The Prior of Cowick 6s

[f.21a]   PARISH OF HOLY TRINITY
Constables John Brygeman, Thomas White and Robert Wytherygge
The store of the said parish church amounts to [blank]

Bowmen able for the war
William Banyan, a bowman, a bow, half sheaf of arrows and is worth in goods 33s 4d
Henry Leche, a bowman, a bow, a pair of gussets, a gorget, a bill and is worth in goods 40s

John Courtes, a bowman, is worth nil
John Mounstephyn, a bowman, harness for a man and is worth in goods £20
Richard Fyncentt, a bowman and is worth in goods 20s
John Andrew, a bowman, a glove of mail and is worth nil
John Paynter, a bowman, servant by the year to Thomas Hyllyng, and is worth nil

Billmen able for the war
Matthew Flete, a stranger born in *Ducheland*, a bill and is worth in goods 40s
John Orchard, a sallet, a bill and is worth in goods 4 marks [40s deleted]
Robert Pygon has no harness and is worth nil
John Oldom, the body of a pair of almain rivets and is worth in goods 40s
John Ley has no harness and is worth in goods 10s

Those not able for the war
John Speke, esq., harness for a man and is worth in goods nil
The same John is seised of tenements and gardens there to the use of *goddyshous* there and is
    worth per annum £3 2s 4d
John Croste is worth in goods £30 18s [£20 deleted]
Robert Alwaye, a breastplate, a bill and is worth in goods nil ESTIMATED
John Uprobyns, a bill and is worth in goods 20s
John Warnegowe, a stranger born in Brittany, servant to the said John Uprobyns, is worth nil
Henry Aysshe is worth in goods 20s
[f.21b] Richard Stubbys, harness for a man and is worth in goods £40 [£10 deleted] ESTIMATED
John Cole [*Exunt* written above] servant to the said Richard, is worth nil
Laurence Polsland, a bow, a half sheaf of arrows and is worth in goods 10s
Oliver Lewys is worth in goods 40s [20s deleted] ESTIMATED
John Poke, a stranger born in Normandy, harness for a man and is worth in goods £20
John Carewe, servant to the said John Poke, is worth nil
Ivon Tracy, a stranger born in Brittany, servant to the said John Poke, is worth nil
Oliver Baloppe, a stranger born in Brittany, is worth nil
John Dotycomb, a stranger born in *Ducheland*, servant to the said Matthew [*sic*] and is worth nil
Derek Venewe, a stranger born in *Ducheland*, servant to the said Matthew [*sic*] and is worth nil
John Morgat, born in Brittany, servant to the same Matthew [*sic*], and is worth nil
John Freys, a stranger born in *Ducheland*, servant to the same Matthew [*sic*], and is worth nil
William Yonge, a bow, a half sheaf of arrows and is worth in goods £4 [60s deleted]
William Bakon, servant to the said William Yonge and is worth nil
Reginald Sadeler, harness for a man and is worth in goods 100s [40s deleted]
Saunder Gryston, apprentice to the said Reginald, and is worth nil
John Bawdon is worth in goods 20s [altered from 10s] ESTIMATED
Thomas Laurent', servant to the said John Bawdon, and is worth nil
Harry Johnson, a stranger born in Brabant, a sallet, an apron of mail, and is worth in goods
    £4 [40s deleted]
Gregory Jane is worth 6s 8d
John Nycoll is worth nil
John Pytforde, a sallet, a halberd and is worth in goods 20s [altered from 10s]
Christopher Haydon, a bill and is worth nil
Thomas Cooper, servant to the said Christopher, is worth in goods 100s [20s deleted]
Margery Hogge, widow, is worth in goods £10 [100s deleted] ESTIMATED
John Cosyn, a halberd and is worth in goods 40s
John Peryn, a bill and is worth nil
John Paterson is worth nil
[f.22a] Thomas Uprobyns is worth in goods 4 marks
Hugh Higgys, a sallet, a bill and is worth in goods £6[1] ESTIMATED
Robert Wetherych, a pair of brigandines, a sallet, a gorget, a fall of mail and a bill and is worth
    in goods £10 [£4 deleted]
Richard Bryndon, a bow, a sheaf of arrows and is worth nil
Hugh Johnson, a stranger is worth nil
John Heryngse, a household servant with the Countess of Devon, a bow, a sheaf of arrows and is
    worth in goods 10 marks [ESTIMATED crossed through in a later hand]
Richard Stycke, a bill and is worth in goods 13s 4d
Alexander Mason is worth nil

1 *Non hic quia in parochia beate marie maioris* written above.

John Dayman, a bill and is worth in goods 23s 4d
Roger Peryham, a bow, a sallet, a half sheaf of arrows and is worth in goods 40s [100s deleted]
Roger Weldow is worth nil
Saunder Dolyn, a bill and is worth 40s
John Newlonde is worth nil
Beatrice Wyllyam, widow, is worth 100 marks [£20 deleted]
James Harres is worth 20s
John Harston, servant to Doctor Norton, harness for a man and is worth 40s
Richard Haukyns, servant to the said John Oldon by the year and is worth nil
Gregory Seyge, harness for a man and is worth 30s
John Humfray is worth nil
Edmund Cheryte is worth nil
John Rawe is worth 10s
Thomas Newton is worth 10s
William Percy is worth 10s [12s deleted]
Harry Marchaunt, a bill and is worth nil
William Wattes is worth nil
Peter Hunte, servant *to my lorde of Excester*, is worth nil ESTIMATED
[f.22b] Thomas Dawe, servant to *my lorde of Wylschere* is worth nil ESTIMATED
William Raynoldes is worth nil ESTIMATED
Roger Wellys is worth 10s
Richard Bray, servant to the said Roger, is worth nil
Thomas Whyte, harness for a man and is worth £20 [altered from £10]
The same Thomas with others is seised of a certain annual rent to the use of the repair of the
    said church 6s 8d
John Salter, a sallet, a pair of splints, a bill and is worth 40s
Harry Vowell is worth 10 marks [40s deleted]
Thomas Archeboll is worth £15 [100s deleted] ESTIMATED
Stephen Grene is worth 10s
John Carowe, harness for 2 men except a pair of splints and is worth 10 marks
Roger Skelton, servant to the said John Carowe and is worth nil
John Spyller, servant to the said John Carowe and is worth nil
William Langcastell is worth nil ESTIMATED
Roger Bayllegh is worth nil
John Grysse, a bill and is worth £4 [40s deleted]
Thomas Hyllyng, a bow, a sheaf of arrows, a halberd and is worth 100s [£4 deleted]
Walter Wescott, servant to *me lorde of Wylschere*, a pair of splints, a sallet, a bill and is worth £7
    [£4 deleted]
Richard Carpynter, a bill and is worth £4 [40s deleted] ESTIMATED
John Browne is worth nil
John Myller, a bow and is worth 10s
Richard Flynt, a bill and is worth 10 marks [100s deleted]
William Thompson, a bill and is worth £3 [40s deleted]
[*John Noseworthy, harness for 2 men and is worth in goods* (blank) entered in a later hand]
[f.23a] [blank] Ducke, doctor of theology, rector of the parish church aforesaid and for his
    benefice there estimated to be worth by the year £12
The same Rector has one tenement there of the annual rent of 12d
Sir Robert Fayreman curate of the same is worth £40 4s 6d [100s deleted]
Sir Thomas Fenton chaplain of *goddyshous* there is worth 6s 8d

Those which have lands in the parish but live outside
Johane Chudlegh, widow, 26s 8d
William Benet and Richard Russell 60s
John Gilbert of Compton Pole, esq., 6s 8d
The Wardens of Exebridge of Exeter 74s
The choristers (*quaresters*) of St Peter of Exeter 20s
William Benet of Exeter 26s 8d
Lady Martha (*Mathena*) Lutterell £9 10s 4d
[blank] Drewe of Torrington, widow, 37s
John Forde of Ashburton 14s
William Takyll 32s
The Dean and Chapter of Exeter 42s 8d

The City of Exeter £5 [£4 16s deleted]
Thomas West, knt., 66s 8d
John Cruygge of Exon 55s 8d
The Prior of Plympton has certain other rents there 12s
[blank] Malerberd of Malmesbury and John Brygman of Exon 30s
[blank] Gyfforde 22s
John Hull of the parish of St Leonard 32s 4d [36s 4d deleted]
Johane Haukyns, widow, 2s
[f.23b] John Ducke of Heavitree 2s 4d
The Prior of St John the Baptist of Exon 16d
Robert Langdon 33s 4d
Otto Gere 3s
Humphrey More 19s [20s deleted]
The Vicars Choral of the Cathedral Church of St Peter of Exon 64s
The Abbot of the House and Church of the blessed Mary of Forde 20s
The Hospital of St Mary Magdalene of Exon 66s
John Somaister of Stokenham 12d
John Sydenham 6s 8d
William Chemallys 23s 4d
Alexander Potell 8s
The Provost of Cambridge 3s
Peter Champenys 23s
John Bydwyll 20s
The Prior of St Nicholas of Exon 5s 8d
[blank] Cayleway in the county of Dorset 16d
The Rector of St Stephen of Exon 6s
Katherine Berdon 56s 8d

[f.24a]   PARISH OF ST GEORGE
Constables John Bridgeman, Matthew Longe and Nigel Colyn
The store of the said parish church amounts to 22d

Bowmen able for the war
Roger Grove, a bow, a half sheaf of arrows and is worth 20s
Simon Horewell, a bow, a sheaf of arrows, a bill and is worth £8 [20 marks deleted]
William Meryfylde, servant to Master William Carant, esq., and is worth nil
John Peter, a bow, a whole harness for a man and is worth £10
Richard Colwyll, a bow, harness for himself and is worth £7 [5 *marks* deleted]

Billmen able for the war
William Hussey, harness for a man and is worth 100 marks [£20 deleted]
Walter Smyth is worth 10s
William Browne, a body of a pair of almain rivets, a bill and is worth 20s
Harry Gele is worth 13s 4d
John Hunte, a bill and is worth 20s
Roger Thorne, a bow, a half sheaf of arrows and is worth 40s [20s deleted]
Maurice Meredeth is worth 13s 4d

Gunners and horsemen
Tristram Hengscott, esq., a horseman harnessed and 2 more men's harness furnished with a bow,
    a sheaf of arrows and a bill, and is worth 100 marks
Stephen Rychard, born in Holland, is worth £3 [20s deleted]
Hugh Cocke, born in Holland, is worth nil
Rowland Harrys, born in Utrecht (*Howtreyght*), is worth nil

Those not able for the war
[*Nicholas Dyxton, chaplain, harness and is worth in goods* £6 entered in a later hand]
[f.24b] Thomas Haycraste is worth nil
Matthew More, harness for a man and is worth £10
William Hull, harness for a man and is worth £10 ESTIMATED
James Toker, a pair of brigandines, a pair of splints, a bill and is worth £6

Robert Flud, a pair of splints, a gorget, a sallet, a bill and is worth £6
John Wolcott, tailor, is worth 10s [*nil* deleted]
Oliver Fullerton is worth 10s ESTIMATED
Derek Fanerys, born in [?] Hesse [*Resse*], is worth nil
Stybye Sadler, born in *Gelderlande*, is worth nil
Richard Cleynger, harness for a man and is worth 100s
Lewis Parkyn, harness for a man and is worth £8 [10 *marks* deleted]
John Haunse, born in Flanders, harness for a man and is worth £20
John Buckram, a pair of brigandines, a sallet, a bill and is worth 20 marks [£10 deleted]
John Peter, servant to the said John, is worth nil
Agnes Copp, widow, is worth £3 [40s deleted] ESTIMATED
Nicholas Copp, a man's harness of mail and is worth 40s
Matthew Longe, harness for a man and is worth £30 [40 *marks* deleted]
John Stott is worth nil
William Bownsham is worth nil
John Olyver, servant to Dame Christine Martyn is worth 20s
Martin Gele, a pole axe and is worth 40s [20s deleted]
John Gele, his son, is worth nil
Guy Blunworth, born in Brittany, is worth 40s [20s deleted]
William Harwod, born in Normandy, is worth 20s
Philip Morys, born in Brittany, apprentice to the said Guy Blunworth, is worth nil
Harry Bowgher, born in Morlaix (*Morles*), is worth nil
Neil Colyn, harness for a man and is worth £20 [20 *marks* deleted]
[f.25a] William Cosyn, servant to William Browne, is worth nil
Stephen Martyn, apprentice to the same William, is worth nil
John Bartlet, tailor, is worth nil
Thomas Benett, servant to Simon Horewell, is worth nil
John Longe, a bill and is worth 40s
Richard Prescott, a bill and is worth 10s
John Marys, 2 men's harness and is worth £20
Richard Veller, harness for a man and is worth £10 [£4 deleted]
John Pryar, servant to the same Richard, is worth nil
William Rugeway, harness for a man and is worth 40s [10s deleted]
John Gybbys, a bill and is worth 20s
Thomas Whytburne, harness for a man and is worth 10s
John Stevyn, a halberd, and is worth 40s
Thomas Baron is worth nil
Thomas Yersye, a bill and is worth 20s
John Romayne, servant to Master Ryse, a bill, a sallet, and is worth nil
William Gowff is worth nil
Margery Santer, widow

Those which have lands within the parish but live outside
The *Lord of St John's* [of Jerusalem] at London 2s 6d
William Peryham 30s
The Dean and Chapter of St Peter's £6 6s
Harry Hamlyn 4 marks
Nicholas Wadham, knt., 48s
John Paynter, 53s 4d
The mother of William Bere of Brushford 26s 8d
John Feer', knt., 53s 4d
[f.25b] Nicholas Longemed £4 9s 4d
The Prior of St John in Exeter 25s 8d
The Mayor and Bailiffs of the City of Exeter 19s 8d
William Benet and Richard Russell 2s 4d
Nicholas Pruscott 3s
John Lanyne 24s 4d
John German 13s 4d
John Fursdon 8s
John Bowdon 16s
Thomas Burnard 20s
Nicholas Wadham, knt., 6s 8d

Roger Blewet 6s
Margery Rugeway 33s 4d
Isabel Fashon 26s 8d
John Hill of *Ogenynges Wyll* 4s
Roger Graynfyld 21s
The Vicars of the Cathedral Church of St Peter 40s
John Marys 26s 8d
John Calwodlegh 55s
The warden of the Hospital of St Mary Magdalene in Exeter 4s
Elinor Drew 46s 8d
John Brodmer' and Richard Andrewe, feoffees to the use of the parish church of St Mary
   Arches in Exeter 23s 4d
Richard Andrewe, Humphrey Andrewe, Henry Hamlyn and John Blackealler 46s 8d

[f.26a] Those which live in the parish and have lands within the same parish
Anys Copp, widow, 12s
Nicholas Copp, 12s
Richard Pruscott 3s
Matthew Longe and Neil Colyn 6s 8d
Sir Richard Vyllayermerii, born in France and parson of the aforesaid parish and his benefice
   is worth by the year £10
Sir Roger Goldsmyth, the parish priest, is worth 40s
Sir William Marys is worth nil

PARISH OF ST DAVID
Constables John Bryckenoll William Ratclyff and William Morys
The store of the said parish church amounts to 26s 8d

Bowmen able for the war
Harry Holonde is worth 40s ESTIMATED
John Hayman, a bow, half a sheaf of arrows, and is worth 20s
Harry Seke is worth nil
William Sowdon is worth nil
John Wallys is worth nil
Thomas Harrys is worth nil

Billmen able for the war
Thomas Davy is worth nil
John Ryxer is worth nil
John Raglonde is worth nil
John Row is worth nil
John Townysyend is worth nil
William Roper is worth nil
[f.26b] Robert Rayshley is worth 20s ESTIMATED
John Crosman is worth nil
Richard Saywarde is worth nil

Those not able for the war
William Ratclyff, harness for 2 men and is worth £100 [*marks* deleted]
Richard Wallys, servant to William Ratclyff, is worth nil
Martin Raymell', servant to the same William, is worth nil
John Smyth, servant to the same William, is worth nil
William Morys, harness for 2 men and is worth £40
John Ley, servant to William Morys, is worth nil
John Howse, a jack, a halberd, and is worth £4
John Efforde, harness for a man and is worth £3 [40s deleted]
Margaret [*William* deleted] Joppe, widow, is worth 40s
Harry Richardes is worth nil
Thomas Beste is worth £4
John Aston is worth 10s
William Monsell, servant to Thomas Stukeley, esq., a bill and is worth 40s

William Clepytt, servant to William Monsell, is worth nil
John Horston is worth nil
William Perewardyn is worth nil
Harry Hayman is worth nil
Robert Peyke is worth 6s 8d
John Sondyfforde is worth 20s [nil deleted]
Thomas Heygons is worth £4 [20s deleted]
John Rowe is worth nil
Richard Perys, a halberd and is worth 13s 4d
John Jaynys is worth nil
Roger Wyllyam is worth nil
Walter Wayle is worth nil
Robert Grenesslade, a bill and is worth 6s 8d [10s deleted]
[f.27a] Richard Jerygo, a sallet and is worth 40s
William More is worth nil ESTIMATED
William Downe is worth 20s
Richard Tayllour is worth nil
Roger Lyghfote is worth nil
Stephen More is worth nil

Those which have lands within the parish but live outside
The Prior of St John's in Exeter £3
The Prior of St Nicholas in Exeter £16 19s 6d
John Symons 26s 8d
John Morys 20s
John Cruygge 19s 4d
The Vicars of St Peter's in Exeter 40s
William Ratclyff 26s 8d
John Noseworthy £3 19s
John Calwodley 10s
The Mayor and Bailiffs of the City of Exeter £50
John Wynter, Richard Varnay and Vincent Scose, feoffees of a will 6s
Richard Pasco, priest, 6s 8d
William Ratclyff and William Morys 13s 10d
Harry Hamlyn and Richard Dixston as feoffees of lands 5s
John Balam 12s
Doctor Norton 18s
John Robyns 10s
Henry Hamlyn 26s 8d
[f.27b] John Calwodley and John Wagott 21s
John German, John Yowe and Robert Fermer as feoffees 8s 6d
John Burgys, John [blank] and David Blake, feoffees, 2s
Geoffrey Lewys and William Mathew, feoffees, 4s 9d
Hugh Yonge of Christow 42s 8d
Giles Hyll £5 3s 3d
John Hull 34s 8d
Walter Pollarde of Plymouth 36s
Thomas Marlo of Ottery St Mary 34s
Edward Specott 9s 9d
John Sydenham of Culmstock £5 11s 4d
John Hexte 5s
John Bustard 16s
Roger Blewet £5 18s 4d
Johane Hawkyns, widow, 8s
Thomas Webyll 10s [10d deleted]
Nicholas Estemonde 7s
Harry Redelake 12s
William Clarke 11s
William Hamont of Bridford 10s 10d
Nicholas [William deleted] Wechals 33s
Dame Elizabeth Larder 20s
My Lady of Pollyslo 12d

Nicholas Wadham, knt., £8 os 2d
John Speke 33s 4d
Thomas Valans, parson of the same parish, for his benefice by the year £7
John Gamonte, the parish priest, is worth 10s

[f.28a]   PARISH OF ST JOHN
Constables Thomas Hodge Peter Downyng and Edward Baberstoke
The store of the said parish church amounts to nil
Henry Duke, Prior of Marsshe and parson of the aforesaid church, for his benefice by the year
    £10

Bowmen able for the war
Thomas Bere, a sallet, a bill and is worth £10
William Goodyng, his servant, is worth nil
[Walter Hoper, a bow, a bill and is worth £10 deleted]
Richard Tayllour is worth 6s 8d
John Vyncant, a bill and is worth nil
William Davy is worth nil
Christopher Brysse is worth nil

Billmen able for the war
William Beryman is worth £12 [£11 deleted]
Stephen Grene, a bill and is worth 13s 4d
John Underhay, a pair of brigandines, a sallet, a bill and is worth £20
Luke Tolmay, a bill, a sallet, standard of mail and is worth 20s
John Sherwode is worth 20s

Those not able for the war
William Burgeyn is worth in goods £19
John Treby, his servant is worth nil
John Loveley, 2 pairs of splints, a sallet, a bill and is worth 20s
John Coleton is worth £4
[f.28b] Henry Kenwode, servant of John Marshall is worth nil
Walter Hoper, a bill, a bow and is worth £10
Peter Shebbrok is worth £6
Roger Kensey, 3 pairs of brigandines with their appurtenances, and is worth £20 ESTIMATED
William Hore, his servant, nil
Thomas Gryott, harness for a man and is worth £10 ESTIMATED
John Marshall, a pair of splints, a coat of mail, a bill, and is worth £16 [20 marks deleted]
Robert Knyth is worth 26s 8d
Roger Syme is worth nil
John Stevyn, a bill and is worth nil ESTIMATED
Philip Bregyn is worth nil
Peter John, born in Guernsey, is worth 10s
Henry Polleman nil
Henry Ector is worth nil
Richard Est, servant to Henry, Earl of Devon, is worth nil ESTIMATED
William Lame is worth nil ESTIMATED
William, his servant, is worth nil
Roger Elyott is worth nil ESTIMATED
Henry Holsdyn is worth nil ESTIMATED
Roger Browne, hat servant to Henry, Earl of Devon, a pair of brigandines and is worth in goods
    nil ESTIMATED
Thomas Syme, a bill and is worth nil
Thomas Caswell is worth 20s
Richard Ratscloff is worth 20s
John May, servant to Mr Alnot Clerke, a pair of brigandines, 2 sallets, 2 bills, a jack and is
    worth 10 marks [£5 deleted]
[f.29a] Thomas Brewer, his servant, is worth nil
Peter Downyng, a pair of brigandines, 3 sallets, a bill, a pole axe and is worth £8 [£10 deleted]

Edward Baburstocke, a pair of almain rivets with 2 pairs of splints and everything pertaining thereto, and is worth £10
John Hall, his servant, is worth nil
William Gruggeworthy, Thomas Lovley, Edward White, servants to J Underhay, nil
Walter Hoper, servant, is worth nil
Margaret Matcotte, widow, is worth 40s
Margaret Gabriell, widow is worth 26s 8d
Thomasine Courteys, widow, is worth 40s
[*Johane White, widow*, £5 deleted]
Johane Keys, widow, is worth 20s
Florence Wardropp, widow, is worth 20s
Elinor Yewons, widow, is worth nil
James Williams, parish clerk, nil

Those that have lands within the parish but live outside
John Speke, with other of the feoffees of Wynard's Almshouse, 34s
The heirs of Thomas Androw £3 18s 6d
William Ruggeway 18s
John Davy of Atherington 54s 4d
The Wardens of the parish church of St Martin £3 8s
William Webber 4s
[f.29b] The Prior of St Nicholas of the aforesaid city 25s 8d
Henry Collen 30s
John Bowdyn 16s 2d
The Prior of St John has by the year 46s
Bery has by the year 20s
The Prior of Totnes 10s
The Mayor and Bailiffs of the City of Exeter 30s
Mistress Hill, widow, 22s 8d
Margaret Weston, widow, 13s 4d
John Jerman 39s
The Countess of Devon 37s 6d
Roger Graynfeld 4s
The Wardens of the parish church of St Olave (*Toly*) 5s 8d
The heirs of Blewytt 48s
John Underhay and John Loveley 8s
Robert Smyth 20s
The Prior of Plympton 6s 8d
John Yong of Bristol 5s 4d
Peter Downyg, Luke Tolmey, [and] John Underhay having an annuity by the year of 7s 2d
Henry Hamlyn, John Whyddon & *other*, in rent by the year 27s 8d
[f.30a] In the store of the Chapel of our Blessed Lady £3 6s 8d
My Lady Larder 18s
John Bere of the South Hams 5s 5½d
William Benett per annum 24s

Aliens
Pascho Tamerett, born in Normandy, is worth nil
Warner Haydon, born in Cologne (*Colen*] is worth 26s 8d
Anthony Peterson, born in Zeeland, a bill, a sallet, a pair of splints and is worth £10

[f.30b] The names of the Canons of the Close of the City of Exeter with their substance

Mr Richard Norton, chanter, is worth in goods 300 marks

The names of his servants
Thomas Styry, a bowman and is worth nil
Thomas Sentlowe, a bowman and is worth nil
Adam Betton, a bowman and is worth nil
Edward Maneryng, a bowman and is worth nil
Richard Yearwode, a bowman and is worth nil
Thomas Tayllour is worth nil

Mr. John Rise, treasurer, is worth in goods [blank]

The names of his servants
Robert Raynold is worth in goods
John Clyff is worth [blank]
Tristram Holond is worth [blank]
Thomas Bonde is worth [blank]

[f.31a] Richard Tollet, archdeacon of Barnstaple is worth £120

The names of his servants
Sir Richard [blank], his chaplain, is worth 60s
William Beamont is worth nil
Thomas Brayynford is worth 20s
John Hogans is worth 40s
Richard Tosard is worth [blank]
William Croke is worth nil
John Dey is worth nil
[blank] Hydley nil
John Coke nil

Mr Robert Weston, subdean is worth 200 marks
Item he has 4 pairs of brigandines

The names of his servants
Sir Peter Maneryng is worth [blank]
Oliver Maneryng is worth £4
William Chechylley is worth 40s
Richard Cotten nil
John Benett is worth nil
Richard Yonge nil
Humphrey Royell is worth nil
John Weston and Thomas Haydon, scholars, are worth nil

[f.31b] Mr Peter Caislegh nothing here because he owes at Wells with his household
Item in harness 2 pairs of brigandines, a coat with eyelet holes [ulet hawlys], with 1 jack, 2 sallets, 2 falls of mail, 2 halberds and a bill

Mr Richard Gilbert is worth £100

The names of his servants
Robert Blewet is worth nil
Christopher Sawnde [and] George Carslegh, scholars, are worth nil
William Quinteryll is worth 26s 8d
Roger Kyllyngworth is worth 40s

Mr Thomas Michell, harness for a man and is worth 200 marks

The names of his servants
Sir Thomas Northbroke is worth 20s
James Michell is worth nil
William Wylkockes is worth 20s
[f.32a] William Coke is worth nil
Bartholomew Garnysche is worth nil
Walter Cock, a scholar, is worth nil

Mr William Horsey is worth [blank]

The names of his servants
John Holbene is worth nil
Philip Howe is worth [blank]
William Bowth is worth [blank]

Richard Gowth is worth [blank]
Giles Horsey, a scholar, [blank]
William Purdey [blank]

Mr George Trevilion, harness for 3 men and is worth 200 marks

The names of his servants
Sir Martin Bewhote is worth nil
Thomas Brodley is worth nil
Robert Harebotell, a billman, is worth nil
John Langmed, a billman, is worth nil
[f.32b] Mr Nicholas Henshewe is worth 100 marks

The names of his servants
Thomas Holond, a bowman, and is worth nil
Geoffrey Eton, a bowman, is worth nil
Henry Henshewe is worth nil
William Webber is worth nil
Thomas Cheswysse is worth nil

Mr Alnot Arescote, a close coat, a sallet, 3 halberds and is worth in goods 200 marks

The names of his servants
John Verney, a bowman, is worth nil
Simon Carewe is worth nil
John Wodefforde is worth nil
Thomas Arescotte, a scholar, is worth nil

Remaining in the fabric chest to the use of the church for the repair of the same and with various
     bonds to the total of £61
Sum total in the church £427 3s
Item remaining in the store of the church for the defence of the same £96 13s 8d

[f.33] The vicars of the same church
Richard Way is worth 10 marks ESTIMATED
John Kenwode is worth 25 marks
John Tregnwyll £20
John Yong nil
Edward Gorgeyn 100s ESTIMATED
John Shebroke 40s
Richard Doke £4 ESTIMATED
Richard Henson 100s
George Wever £4
William Danson £4
William Rode £4
Richard Bynkes 4 marks
John Perker 40s
Robert Phylypp 40s
Roger Wytton is worth nil
John Tolmey nil
William Spile nil
John Wylkynson 13s 4d
Thomas Downe 40s
Robert Dyxton nil

[f.33b] Annuellers
John Maior is worth £10
John Aylesmor' is worth £4
Robert Hurston is worth £4
William Longe is worth 100s
Michael Cruse is worth 25 marks
John Hornebroke is worth £10

John Prill is worth £10
John Kyttow is worth £8
James Tremelyon is worth £8
Richard Coner is worth 60s
John Drake 100s
Richard Smyth £8
John Eyrmewe is worth £7
Thomas Hewett 20 marks
William Dyer £4
Nicholas Bolter £4
Charles Stopfford *altasta* of Mr John Speke 100s
John Hampton *altasta* of Sir John de Grandissone £20

[f.34a] *Secundarii*
William Huchyns is worth nil
George Sherwyll 10 marks
George Squyer nil
John Burnerd is worth 40s
William Cane is worth £4
Thomas Wynforde is worth nil
Thomas Carter is worth nil
Humphrey Byre is worth nil
Thomas Helston nil
John Trigges is worth 5 marks
Robert Bulhed is worth £7
William Tanner is worth nil
[ff. 34b and 35a blank]
[f.35b] Mr Bure £20
Mr M. German £10
[ff. 36a–38b blank and ff. 39a–41a contain material not relevant to the assessment]
[f.41b] [Notes of some payments made, but entries crossed through]
The wedow in northin stret
Skydmore
the petty collectors to be chossyn
Ryc Swet & Henry Mawnder
          collectons [*sic*]

THE SUBSIDY OF 1524/5

[m.1 Abstract of heading] The estreat and certificate made 31 March 15 Henry VIII [1524] by John Symon, mayor, Richard Duke, John Bradmore and John Noseworthy, four of the King's Commissioners for the collection of the subsidy granted to the King at the last parliament, to the Barons of the Exchequer for the account to be taken of John Brycknoll, authorised for the receiving of the money on the first collection and payment of the subsidy from the persons and parishioners within the said city and suburbs of the same, and paying it into the Exchequer, as follows.

[m.2]   PARISH OF ST LAWRENCE

John Calwodley for goods	£50	50s		Thomas Schere for wages	40s	12d
Richard Vernay for				John Northbroke senior		
goods	200 marks £6 13s 4d			for goods	£6	3s
Thomas Hunte for goods[1]	£40	40s		Robert Newlonde for		
[?Robert] Frear for				goods	40s	12d
goods	£18	9s		John Wynter for goods	£20	20s
John M . . . for goods	40s	12d		William Petty for goods	£20	20s
John Harvy for goods	£8	4s		John Sheffyld for goods	£20	20s
John Person for wages	20s	4d		George Abell for goods	40s	12d
John Chapley for wages	20s	4d		William Corant for wages	20s	4d
Thomas Glamfeld for				Vincent Scosse for goods	£20	20s
goods	£6	3s		Robert Browne for goods	40s	12d
John Kever for wages	20s	4d		Nicholas Gervys for wages	20s	4d
William Lympyn for				Henry Luter for goods	£10	5s
wages	20s	4d		William Mays for wages	26s 8d	4d
Richard Barbor for goods	40s	12d		Robert Bayle for wages	33s 4d	4d
Henry Brewyster for				Robert Harward for		
goods	£4	2s		wages	33s 4d	4d
William Lobdon for wages	40s	12d		Johane Lympeny for		
William Baker for wages	20s	4d		goods	. . .	4d
John Conet for wages	20s	4d		John Clarke for goods	£3	18d
Thomas Stevyn for wages	20s	4d		[blank] Perys for wages	26s 8d	4d
Thomas Torryn for wages	20s	4d		William Freys for wages	40s	12d
John Bretyn, carver,				[blank] servant to Robert		
alien, for wages	20s	12d		Dolle for wages	20s	4d
John Scherman for goods	40s	12d				
Richard Yeme for wages	20s	4d				
William Clerke for wages	20s	4d		PARISH OF ST STEPHEN		
John Colman for goods	£20	20s		. . . Page for goods	£100	100s
William Whyte for				. . . Holmore junior for		
goods[2]	£20	20s		goods	£40	40s
Thomas Cokeram for				. . . Chalmore and other		
goods	£3	18d		children of John		
Richard Lentall for				Cholmer for goods	£40	
goods	40s	12d		. . .ke for goods	£100	
John Snellyng for goods	£16	8s		. . .		
Richard Dolle for goods	£7	3s 6d		John Bodley		
Henry Drewe for wages	26s 8d	4d		. . .		
John Stevyn for wages	20s	4d		. . .		

[1] See Appendix 1.
[2] *Bill'* in margin. *xvˢquo debet* . . . written by side of total.

35

[m.3] Roger Whyte for goods £10   5s
William Peryman for goods £4   2s
John Caster for wages 40s   12d
Nicholas Sperke for wages 20s   4d
Michael Pepyn, alien, for goods 40s   2s
Robert Turner for goods 20 marks   6s 6d
Peter Spryng for goods £6 13s 4d   3s
Richard Coke for goods 10 marks   3s . . .
Thomas Balard for wages 20s   4d
William Coloff, alien, for wages 20s   12d
John Clement for wages . . .
Mary Fyesse *hath landys by the yere* £4   4s
John Crowdecott for wages 20s   4d
Lawrence [blank] for wages 20s   . . .d
William Huchyns for goods 40s   12d
Peter Cosyn for wages 20s   4d
Richard Hert for goods £10   5s
Robert Bysschopp for wages 20s   4d
Matthew Cobleghe for goods 4 marks   12d
William Wekys for goods £4   2s
Nicholas Rutter for goods £10   5s
John Growode for wages 40s   12d
John Waryn for wages 20s   4d
Ralph Roddon for wages 20s   4d
Richard Lymery for wages 20s   4d
William Barbour for goods 20s   4d
Thomas Apryse for goods 20s   4d
James Rodys for goods £6   3s
Richard Fooke for wages 20s   4d
Simon Carewe for wages 26s 4d   4d
John Hayne . . . 40s   12d
John Hawkyn for wages 20s   . . .
John Whyte for wages 20s   4d
Bernard Johnson, alien, for wages 20s   12d
Thomas Richardes for wages 20s   4d

PARISH OF ST MARTIN
John Scosse for goods £100   100s
Geoffrey Lewys for goods £40   40s
Nicholas Lymet for goods £50   50s
Nicholas Halle for wages 20s   . . .
Martin Queffyn, alien, for goods £7   7s
John Shappe, alien, for wages 30s   . . .
William Davy for goods 100s   2s 6d

Gilbert Waryn for goods £6 13s 4d   3s
William Peke for goods £40   30s . . .
Thomas Bevesiter for goods £6   3s
John Damalens, alien, for wages 20s   . . .
Richard Senthyll *habet* . . . £7   7s
Henry Cutberd for wages 20s   4d
William Tothyll for goods £10   5s
Stephen Smyth for wages 20s   . . .
John Hals for goods 40s   12d
Richard Brendon for goods 40s   12d
Thomas Dawe for goods £5   2s 6d
Stephen Preston for wages 33s 4d   . . .
Richard H. . . for wages 20s   4d
Peter Johnson, alien, for wages 20s   4d
John Johnson for wages 20s   4d
John Broke for goods £6   3s
William Bevercomb, alien, for wages 20s   12d
Stephen Lorymer for goods £7   3s 6d
William Laurens for wages 36s 8d   . . .d
Thomas Geare for wages 20s   . . .d
[m.4] Marian Hyllersdon in lands and tenements £4   4s
John Holmore senior for goods 40 . . .
Edward Voysy for wages £3   18d
Henry Moke for goods 100s   2s 6d
Nicholas Baton for wages 20s   . . .
Peter Chanderby, alien, for wages xx . . .
Thomas Courtys for goods £4   2s
Johane Daymond, widow, for goods 40s   12d
Margery Panter for lands £3   3s
Thomas Monday for wages 20s   4d
Henry Hensthow for wages 26s 8d   4d
Thomas Phelypp for wages 26s 8d   4d
John Rogers for wages 26s 8d   4d
John Coker for wages 26s 8d   4d
Thomas Honde for wages 40s   12d
Vitallus Ford for wages 20s   4d
John Holbem for wages 40s   12d
Philip Howe for wages 26s 8d   4d
James Walker for wages 26s 8d   4d
Richard Gogh for wages 26s 8d   4d
William Chucheley for wages 26s 8d   4d
Oliver Manneryng for wages 40s   12d

Richard Cottyn for		
wages	26s 8d	4d
John Benet for wages	20s	4d
James More for wages	20s	4d
Simon Carowe for		
wages	nothing here	
	because he owes in	
	the parish of St.	
	Stephen	
William Demond for		
wages	20s	4d
John Sergant for wages	26s 8d	4d
John Holman for wages	33s 4d	4d
Richard Lybbe for wages	36s 8d	4d
Gilbert Asthley for wages	26s 8d	4d
John Chechir' for wages	26s 8d	4d
Alex [blank] for wages	26s 8d	4d
Bawdon [blank] for wages	20s	4d
Philip [blank] for wages	40s	12d
William Webber for		
goods	26s 8d	4d
Thomas Haulle for		
wages	33s 4d	4d
William Raynol for		
wages	33s 4d	. . .
Richard Morman for		
wages	33s 4d	4d

PARISH OF ST PAUL

Richard Chubbe for		
goods	£40	40s
Johane Wellys, widow,		
for goods	£40	40s
Richard Hopkyns for		
wages	40s	12d
William Penycott for		
wages	26s 8d	4d
Thomas Tuckefyld, brewer,		
for goods	£20	20s
Thomas Gagge for wages	20s	4d
John Bartlet, carrier,		
for goods	£20	20s
Thomas More for wages	30s	. . .
Robert Raysley for		
wages	40s	12d
Johane Hull, widow,		
for goods	£10	5s
Richard Lorymer for		
goods	20 marks	6s 6d
Thomas Heth for goods	£8	4s
Ellis Harrys for wages	30s	4d
Daniel Densforde for		
wages	26s 8d	4d
Robert Wescott for goods	£4	2s
John Russell for wages	40s	12d
Richard Hyll for wages	26s 8d	4d
Richard Brownemed for		
goods	£4	2s
Richard Taillour for		
goods	40s	12d
Johane Farewell for goods	£4	2s

John Raglonde for		
goods	40s	12d
Robert Condet for wages	20s	4d
[m.5] Nicholas Sporyer for		
wages	20s	4d
Simon Edwardes for		
wages	20s	4d
David Drake for wages	20s	4d
John Maunsell for wages	. . .	12d
John Prowse for wages	40s	12d
John Abaprystevell for		
wages	26s 8d	4d
John Trott for wages	26s 8d	4d
William Lystoyll for		
wages	20s	4d
John Hewys for goods	40s	12d
John Cannyng for wages	20s	4d
John Browne, currier,		
for wages	20s	4d
Thomas Trevyll for goods	40s	12d
William Davy for goods	40s	12d
Alison Cooke for goods	40s	12d
John Walker for wages	20s	4d
Richard Bayly for wages	20s	4d
Edmund Gropyll for		
wages	4cs	12d
Peter Scher, alien, for		
goods	£4	4s
Hugh Poppe for wages	40s	12d
Nicholas Rutte, alien,		
for wages	20s	12d

PARISH OF ALL HALLOWS GOLDSMITH STREET

John Schelder for goods	£40	40s
John Yeow, bowyer,		
for goods	£120	£6
John Nycholles for goods	£40	40s
John Vylfayne for goods	£40	40s
John Germyn for goods	40 marks	26s
Andrew Mannyng for		
goods	20 marks	6s 6d
Robert Deryng for wages	20s	4d
Henry Ducheman for		
wages	52s	2s . . .
Peter Moste, alien, for		
wages	40s	2s
Derek Gossam, Dutchman,		
for wages	40s	2s
Roger Galsworthy for		
wages	20s	4d
John Drewe for wages	20s	4d
Margaret Golde, widow,		
for goods	20s	4d
Nicholas Abell for wages	20s	4d
John Carter for goods	£10	5s
Robert Pewer for wages	40s	12d
John Northbroke junior		
for goods	£10	5s
James Brewer, Dutchman,		
for wages	20s	12d

Robert Robelet, alien, for wages	20s	12d
John Dyer for wages	20s	4d
Robert Marche for goods	£3	18d
John Lane for goods	£20	20s
John Rychard for goods	£4	2s
John Cotte for wages	20s	4d
Robert Fermer for goods	£6	3s
Roger [blank] for wages	20s	4d
William Stevyns for goods	20 marks	6s
Thomas Olyver for goods	£10	5s
Hugh Warde for wages	40s	12d
Richard Murthe for goods	40s	12d
Anthony Water, Dutchman, for wages	20s	8d
John Mysse for wages	20s	4d
John Cowley for wages	20s	4d

PARISH OF ST PANCRAS

William Symons for goods	£20	20s
John Bocher for wages	£20	...
Oliver Parre for goods	...	
[m.6] John Harte for lands	£4	4s
... ys for goods	40s	12d
... for wages	33s 4d	4d
... for goods	£4	2s
... for goods	£10	5s
...	...	2s 6d
...	20s	4d
... for wages	50s	12d
... for goods	£10	5s
... for goods	£30	30s
... widow, for goods	100s	2s 6d
... for wages	20s	4d
... *chylderyn* of John Thomas for goods	£10	5s

PARISH OF ST KERRIAN

Anna Crugge, widow, for goods	400 marks	20 marks 1s[1]
Lancelot Harnage for goods	£20	20s
Christopher Mixstowe for goods	20 marks	6s 6d
William Massy for goods	100s	2s 6d
David Blake for wages	20s	4d
William Burgys for goods	£6	3s
John Martyn for wages	30s	4d
John Dinise for goods	40s	12d
William Wylliams for wages	20s	4d
... More for wages	20s	4d
... Drake	20s	4d

[1] *et . . . 5 mar . .*

... Wyllyams ...	20s	4d

[document defective: approximately 12 names missing]

PARISH OF ST PETROCK

Peter Strache for goods	£100	100s
William Buckyngham for goods	£50	50s
John Bricknoll for goods	£300	£15 5s ...
Robert Buller for goods	£200 41s	10½ marks
John Wynter for goods	£40	40s
John More for goods	£100	100s
John Wolcott, merchant, for goods	£40	40s
John Symon, esq., for goods	£100	100s
John Thomas for goods	£40	40s
Richard Martyn for goods[1]	£66 13s 4d	£3 6s 8d
John Buller for goods	200 marks	£6 13s 4d
William Hurste for goods[2]	£200	£10...
Thomas Hunte for goods	200 marks	10 marks
Richard Hunt for goods	£30	30s
[m.7] John Robyns son of John Robyns	£18	9s
Thomas Robyns son of said John	£18	9s
John Dayman for wages	53s 4d	12d
Thomas Provest for goods	£10	5s
Richard Smyth for goods	£8	4s
Thomas Sandyford for wages	26s 8d	4d
Margaret Bucknan, widow, for goods	£20	20s
William Dobyns for lands	£3	3s
John Scoytt for goods	40s	12d
Thomas Fuller for goods	£20	20s
John Docke for goods	£20	20s
Henry Bestatour, alien, for goods	£6	6s
Ralph Furnansse for wages	33s 4d	4d
Richard Benaker for wages	26s 8d	4d
William Gomby for goods	40s	12d
William Comyn for wages	20s	4d
Thomas Stevyn for wages	20s	4d
Edward Shere for goods	£6 13s 4d	3s
John Wynter, tailor, for wages	20s	4d
Ivan Codlyn, alien, for goods	£4	4s

[1] *Bill'* in margin. See Appendix I.
[2] See Appendix I.

John Burlace for goods	£10	5s
Edward Hylman for goods	£4	2s
Robert Northbroke for goods	£10	5s
William Chanons for goods	£8	4s
William Seldon for goods	40s	12d
Richard Denys for goods	40s	12d
John Whyte for goods	40s	12d
Agnes Hoke for goods	40s	12d
Johane Cardmaker for goods	40s	12d
John Purser for wages	40s	12d
Hugh Delaker for goods	4cs	12d
John Wodeber' for goods	£6	3s
Thomas Abell for wages	40s	12d
Leonard Thomas for goods	40s	12d
John Wagott for goods	£8	4s
John Wylcoke for wages	20s	4d
John Tuckefylde, tailor, for goods	£4	2s
Thomas Androw for wages	40s	12d
Johane Baker, widow, for goods	40s	12d
Robert Hele for wages	40s	12d
Thomas Sweytlonde for wages	40s	12d

PARISH OF ST MARY ARCHES

John Bradmore for goods	10 marks	1s[1]
John Maynard for goods	£40	40s
Gilbert Kyrke for goods	300 marks	£10
Richard Andrewe for goods	£200	£10
John Blackaller for goods	£200	£10
Christopher Lamberd for goods	£100	100s
William Forest for goods	£40	40s
John Amore for goods	£40	40s
John Waye for goods £100	101s	£3 10s[2]
Robert Smyth for goods	£50	50s
William Alyn for goods	100s	2s 6d
Hugh Davy for goods	£10	5s
John Cowyke for wages	30s	8d
Richard Faux for goods	50 marks	33s 4d
John Ketylton for goods	£3	18d
Thomas Bonyfaunt for goods	£10	5s
David Neyll for wages	26s 8d	4d
Richard Dowell for wages	nil quia habet . . . quia est impotens	

Robert Smyth junior for wages	20s	4d
Elizabeth Gervys, widow, in lands and tenements per annum	20s	12d
Richard Burnyng for goods	£3	18d
William Brigge for goods	£3	18d
Richard Mawdyt for goods	40s	12d
Richard Chemney for wages	26s 8d	4d

[m.8] PARISH OF ST OLAVE

Roger Luxston for goods	£110	110s
Thomas Hoygge for goods	£200	£10
Henry Hamlyn for goods[1]	£200	£10[2]
Thomas Harrys for goods	£200	£10
William Peryham for goods	£200	£10
William Underhay for goods	£3	18d
William Meryfyld for wages	20s	4d
Nicholas Rayne for wages	20s	4d
John Cradocke for goods	£6	3s
William Gyldon for goods	40s	12d
Thomas Rede for goods	£10	5s
John Strobrigge for lands and tenements	£4	4s
William Wygsted for goods	40s	12d
John Symon for goods	40s	12d
John Kent for goods	40s	12d
James Tyat for goods	40s	12d
John . . . for wages	. . .s	4d
. . . for goods	. . .	xvjd
[document defective: possibly two names missing]		
Robert . . .		
Robert Petr. . .		
John [blank] . . .		
Richard Bery for goods	40s	12d
John Treve for goods	20s	4d
William Drayton for goods[3]	£20	20s
Laurence Pollyslond for goods	40s	12d
Robert Cottener for goods	£7	3s 6d
William Wylson for goods	20s	4d
Richard Swyte for goods	40s	12d

[1] *et sic debet ut per billam x marks*, written above.
[2] *bill'* in margin.

[1] *bill'* in margin.
[2] *solvet x marks et sic debet v marks pro billa*
[3] See Appendix I.

Thomas Hanke for wages	nil	
John Whydon for goods	£10	5s
Thomas Ryder for wages	40s	12d
Richard Brokyn' for wages	nil	

PARISH OF ST JOHN

William Burgoyn for goods	£19	9s 6d
John Marshall for goods	£16	8s
John Collyton for wages	43s 4d	13d
John Loveley for goods	40s	12d
Thomas Bere for goods	£10	5s
William More for wages	30s	4d
William Goddyng for wages	40s	12d
Robert Knyght for goods	40s	12d
Thomas Smyth for wages	20s	4d
Luke Tolmaye for goods	£4	2s
[*John Potter for wages*, deleted]		
Thomas Gryott for goods	£7	3s 6d
Walter Hoper for goods	£10	5s
Robert Bresse for wages	30s	4d
Robert John for wages	30s	4d
Edmund Wetcomb for wages	20s	4d
John Radman for wages	40s	12d
Robert Davy for wages	40s	12d
John Scherwod for goods	40s	12d
John Water for wages	30s	4d
Lewis Sage for goods	£3	18d
Robert Frer' for goods	40s	12d
Richard Bendon for goods	£3	18d
John Underhay for goods	£20	20s
John Vyncent for goods	40s	12d
Roger Syme for wages	20s	4d
Peter John for wages	20s	4d
[m.9] Thomas Thomas for wages	20s	4d
Thomasia Courtes, widow, for goods	40s	12d
William Lambe for wages	20s	4d
John Stevyn for wages	20s	4d
Richard Rowe for wages	20s	4d
Philip Bregan for goods	40s	12d
Thomas Carswyll for goods	40s	12d
Roger Kensey for goods	£20	20s
John May for goods	£6 13s 4d	3s . . .
William Beryman for goods	£12	6s
Peter Downyng for goods	£8	4s
Edward Baverstoke for goods	£10	5s
William Davy for wages	20s	4d
Anthony Peterson, alien, for goods	£10	10s
Margaret Matcot, a Scot, for goods	40s	2s
Michael Cholwayt, alien, for wages	20s	12d

Pascow Tymaret, alien, for wages	20s	12d
Bernard Haydon, alien, for goods	100s	5s
Robert Fresse, alien, for wages	40s	2s
William Hore for wages	20s	4d
John Geyll, servant to Bavurstocke, for wages	20s	4d

PARISH OF ALL HALLOWS ON THE WALLS

Ralph Martyn for goods	100s	2s 6d
John Garlond for wages	20s	4d
William Carow for goods	20s	4d
John Bugbroke for goods	£10	5s
Richard Colyn for goods	40s	12d
John Faux for goods	40s	12d
Thomas Martyn for wages	20s	4d
Richard Harrys for wages	20s	4d
John Alyn for wages	20s	4d
John Tyncam for goods	20s	4d
Walter Gaydon for goods	£3	18d
Robert Lane for wages	20s	4d
Nicholas Martyn for wages	20s	4d
William Musdon for wages	20s	4d
Thomas Davy for goods	40s	12d
William Leche for wages	20s	4d
Thomas Rychardes for goods	100s	2s 6d
Stephen More for goods	40s	12d
Nicholas Paxe for wages	20s	4d
Oliver Breton for wages	20s	12d

PARISH OF ST MARY STEPS

William Radforde for goods	40s	12d
Agnes Fox, widow, for goods	40s	12d
John Bartlet for goods	£6 13s 4d	3s
John Mussell for wages	20s	4d
John Dunse for wages	20s	4d
John Horewode for goods	40s	12d
Richard Erlonde for wages	20s	4d
John Cockehyll for wages	20s	4d
James Bery for goods	£4	2s
Henry Holway for wages	20s	4d
William Cottyforde for goods	40s	12d
John Saye for goods	£4	2s
William Robyns for wages	20s	4d
William Rolffe for wages	20s	4d
Robert Talboytt for goods	40s	12d
John Martyn for goods[1]	£20	20s . . .
William Clyff for wages	20s	4d
John Turner for wages	20s	4d
John Jooll for goods	20s	4d
John Scobhyll for wages	20s	4d

[1] See Appendix I.

[The entries for the following parishes are from the 1525 assessment, that for 1524 being defective.]

PARISH OF ST GEORGE

. . . for goods	100s	2s 6d
Agnes . . . for goods	100s	2s 6d
Henry Hamlyn for goods	£100	100s
John Trubody for goods	£40	40s
Thomas Chamberlayne, *korser*	100s	2s 6d
William Hull for goods	20 marks	6s 8d
John [blank], servant, for wages	30s	4d
Richard Claynger for goods	£10	5s
Johane Parkyng, widow, for goods	£10	5s
John [blank], servant, for wages	33s 4d	4d
Robert Pomerey for goods	£10	5s
John Pyn' for wages	20s	4d
Richard Est for wages	20s	4d
William Poyle for wages	20s	4d
Roger Thorn, hellier, for goods	40s	12d
John Hunt for wages	20s	4d
Thomas Boyle for goods	20s	4d
John Smeth for wages	20s	4d
John Baker for goods	100s	2s 6d
Thomas Whyteborn for goods	£4	2s
John Gybbys for goods	40s	12d
John Pyter, tucker, for goods	£20	20s
William Rugeway for goods	40s	12d
Richard Veller for goods	20 marks	6s 8d
John [his] servant, for wages	20s	4d
William Torner, pin-maker, for goods	30s	4d
Richard Calle for goods	20s	4d
John Paynter, shoemaker, for wages	20s	4d
John Lange, butcher, for goods	40s	12d
Simon Horwyll, baker, for goods	£10	5s
John [his] servant, for wages	20s	4d
Henry Well for wages	40s	12d
William Browne for goods	40s	12d
Neil Colyng for goods	£20	20s
Gey Allyn for wages	£3	18d
Martin Gale for goods £6 13s 4d		3s 4d
John [blank], servant, for wages	20s	4d
John Jakes, alien, for wages	26s 8d	8d

Matthew Longe for goods	£30	30s
John [blank], his servant, for wages	40s	12d
Nicholas Coppe for goods	10 marks	3s 4d
John, his servant, for wages	20s	4d
Agnes Coppe, widow, for goods	40s	12d
Agnes Bocram, widow, for goods	£10	5s
Hans Pekylheryng, alien, for goods	£20	40s
John, his servant, for wages	40s	12d
Tristan Henskott for goods [1]	£100	£5
Oliver Folverton, pewterer, for wages	30s	4d
[blank] Wulcott for wages	30s	4d
John Olyver for wages	20s	4d
Maude West, widow, for goods	nil	
Robert Flodde, tailor, for goods	£5	2s 6d
Richard Colwyll for goods	10 marks	3s 4d
John, his servant, for wages	33s 4d	4d
James Tocker for goods	nil	
William . . . for goods 40 marks		26s 8d
John Morys for goods	£20	20s
Total £24 17s		

PARISH OF ST DAVID

John . . . for goods	100s	2s 6d
Richard Jer. . . for goods	£4	2s
Thomas Hochyns for goods	£4	2s
John Ivere for goods	£4	2s
John Raglond for wages	20s	4d
John Hayman for wages	40s	14d
John Daniell for wages	30s	4d
John Sandford for wages	40s	12d
Edmund Hayman for wages	20s	4d
Thomas Walys for wages	40s	12d
John Townson for wages	20s	4d
Richard Seward for wages	20s	4d
John Crosseman for wages	20s	4d
Ralph Androw for wages	20s	4d
Harry Hayman for wages	20s	4d
Richard Walys for wages	40s	12d
Richard Retenbery for wages	40s	12d
John Quetrell for wages	20s	4d
Richard Peke for wages	40s	12d
Robert Grenslade for wages	30s	4d
John Rowe for wages	20s	4d

[1] See Appendix I

John Ayston for wages	20s	4d
John Lake for wages	40s	12d
Roger Lyzthfote for wages	nil	
William Coper for wages	40s	12d
John Waye for wages	20s	4d
John Ryxer for wages	20s	4d
William Gend for wages	20s	4d
John Raffe for wages	20s	4d
Robert Raschle for wages	20s	4d
Laurence Hancoke for wages	20s	4d
Thomas Beste for goods	£4	2s
William Rattcleffe for goods	£100	£5
William Takell for goods	£40	40s
John Mauncell for goods	40s	12d
Total £8 5s 6d		

PARISH OF ST. MARY MAJOR

Henry Clerke for goods	40s	12d
John Cheryton for goods	£10	5s
Philip Garret for goods [1]	£18	9s
Thomas Harrys, his servant, for wages	33s 4d	4d
. . . Bebyry for goods	40s	12d
Benet Glubbe for goods	£3	18d
John Alyn for goods	£5	2s 6d
John Peyter for goods	£10	5s
Henry Coke for wages	26s 8d	4d
William Coblond for goods	20s	4d
Eleanor Partrigge, widow, for goods	40s	12d
Thomas Layghay, capper, for goods	20s	4d
Walter Rondell for goods	£15	. . .
Peter, his servant, alien, for wages	40s	2s
Thomas Clark, his servant, for wages	33s 4d	4d
Richard Basset for goods	£20	. . .
John Davy for goods	20s	4d
John Waytt *alias* Symon for goods	40s	12d
William Albrigth for goods	20s	4d
John Smyth for goods	£4	2s
William Benet for goods	40 marks	26s 8d
John Rypley for goods	40 marks	26s 8d
William Voysey for goods	10 marks	3s 4d
Robert Toker for goods	20 marks	6s 8d
William Smyth, goldsmith, for goods	30s	4d
Jelys Skynner, a Breton, for wages	26s 8d	4d
Cleoffas Harvy, Breton, for goods	40s	12d

[1] See Appendix I, where name is given as John Garett.

John, his servant, for wages	40s	12d
John Umfray for goods	40s	12d
Oliver Bregard, Breton, for wages	40s	12d
Thomas Haukyns for wages	40s	12d
William Amysse, tailor, for goods	20s	4d
Walter Howell at Corner for goods	£18	10s
Walter Parre for wages	40s	12d
Henry Birde for wages	40s	12d
Richard Jamys for wages	40s	12d
Alice Brigeman for goods [1]	£40	40s
Richard Eliott, her servant, for wages	20s	4d
Edward Briggeman for goods	£6	3s
Edward Daylond for goods	£20	20s
Walter Trotte for goods	10 marks	3s 4d
Hugh Hygges for goods	£20	20s
Robynett le Jaunder for goods	40s	12d
Thomas Cotten for goods	£10	5s
John Whytffyld for goods	20 marks	6s 8d
Edmund Gee, his servant, for wages	40s	12d
Henry Jewll, a Breton, for wages	20s	8d
John Polleslond for goods	100s	2s 6d
William Kyng, a Breton, for wages	40s	2s
Richard Smerte for wages	20s	4d
. . . Olyver, a Breton, for wages	20s	8d
John Bonefaunt for goods	10 marks	3s 4d
Robert Northway for goods	40s	12d
Richard Avere for goods	40s	12d
Rowland Gelytt worth	nil	
Amys William worth	20s	4d
Thomas Stephyn, weaver, worth	5 marks	20d
Roger . . . for goods	20s	4d
John Cornysshe for goods	nil	
Robert Lane for goods	20s	4d
John Smyth for goods	40s	12d
. . . for goods	5 marks	20d
. . . hanger for goods	10 marks	3s 4d
Nicholas . . .	20s	4d
John . . . for goods	20s	4d
John . . . for goods	20s	4d
. . .	5 marks	20d
. . .	5 marks	20d

[1] See Appendix I.

. . . for wages	nil	
. . . for goods	£6	3s
. . .	40s	12d
. . . Bowforest worth	£4	2s
John Dyxton for goods	5 marks	20d
John, his servant, for		
wages	30s	. . .
. . . for goods	£40	. . .
. . . for wages	26s	. . .
John Dyxton, servant to		
Richard Dyxton	20s	4d
. . .ke for wages	26s 8d	4d
. . .	20s	4d
. . . for goods	20s	8d
. . .	40s	12d
. . .	£4	2s
. . . for wages	52s	14d
John . . ., apprentice,		
worth	20s	8d
Raffe P. . . for lands	40s	2s
. . . Bal. . . for goods	£10	5s
. . . for wages	33s 4d	4d
. . . for goods	£6	3s
Laurence, his servant,		
Breton apprentice	20s	8d
John Damsell for goods	£20	20s
William Hotte for goods	£6	3s
John Grosse for wages	20s	4d
Alice Isacke for wages	20s	4d
Geffra Pomfreytt for goods	£4	2s
William Sommester		
for goods	40 marks	26s 8d
John Trenchard for		
goods	20s	4d
Hugh Stamperd for		
wages	33s 4d	4d
Walter Howell the		
longer for goods	£20	20s
Richard Graygh for		
wages	40s	12d
John Pope for wages	26s 8d	4d
William Sall for wages	40s	12d
Benet Horne for wages	40s	12d
Robert Hoker for goods	£40	40s
John Keyth for goods	53s 4d	16d
John Deram, a Breton,		
his apprentice	20s	8d
John Vall for goods	£4	2s
John Fyne for goods	20s	4d
Richard Yong for goods	20s	4d
Thomas Sterre, servant to		
Mr Tresorer, for		
wages	26s 8d	4d
Adam Betton for wages	26s 8d	4d
Thomas Taillour for		
wages	26s 8d	4d
John Mornyng, his servant,		
for wages	26s 8d	4d
James Michell, servant with		
doctor Michell, for wages	40s	12d
John Crosse for wages	26s 8d	4d
John Sotheres for wages	26s 8d	4d

Maurice Abbeyr for		
wages	26s 8d	4d
Nicholas Chalcross,		
servant [to] Mr		
Archedeken, for goods	£10	5s
Christopher Harrys, butler		
of Calonderhay, for		
wages	26s 8d	4d
[blank] Davy, Clerk of		
Seynt Mary Michell,		
for wages	26s 8d	16d
George Dudley, servant		
to lord byschoppe, for		
wages	53s 4d	16d
Gawen Carew for wages	53s 4d	16d
William Gyfford for		
wages	53s 4d	16d
Thomas Foster for wages	53s 4d	16d
William Yong for wages	53s 4d	16d
Thomas Gybbons for		
wages	53s 4d	16d
John Yeard for wages	53s 4d	16d
Nicholas Strowt for wages	40s	12d
James Staveyley for		
wages	40s	12d
John Cole for wages	40s	12d
William Barbour for		
wages	40s	12d
Henry Hensthow for		
wages	40s	12d
William Chamber for wages	40s	12d
Nicholas Bartlett for		
wages	40s	12d
John Lynde for wages	40s	12d
Robert Coke for wages	40s	12d
Thomas Phelips for		
wages	40s	12d
Henry Arowsmyth for		
wages	40s	12d
Raffe Mustarde for wages	26s 8d	4d
Roger Cartwreyth for		
wages	26s 8d	4d
John Rosse for wages	26s 8d	4d
James Artur for wages	26s 8d	4d
John Bevy for wages	40s	12d
Geoffrey Peryns for wages	40s	12d
Clement for wages	40s	12d
Roger Colter for goods	40 marks	26s 8d
Total £25 15s 2d		

PARISH OF HOLY TRINITY

[m.4a] Eleanor Speke,		
widow, for goods	nil hic quia onerat	
	in Co[m] . . .	
John Crofton for goods	£26	26s
Robert Alway for lands	£8	8s
Henry Aysche for goods	40s	12d
Richard Stubbys for goods[1]	£16	8s
John Humfray, alien, in		
in pledges	26s 8d	8d

[1] See Appendix I.

Name	Amount	Tax
John Norseworthy for goods	£40	40s
William Tolslo for wages	nil	
Robert [blank] for wages	nil	
Margery Burgh, widow, for goods	40s	12d
Oliver Lewys for wages	40s	12d
John Poke, denizen, for goods	£6 13s 4d	3s 4d
Thomas [blank] for wages	20s	4d
Richard Axe for wages	20s	4d
Ivan Tracey, alien, for wages	20s	8d
William Yonge, barber, for goods	100s	2s 6d
Christopher Haydon for goods	40s	12d
Margery Hoigge, widow, for goods	£10	5s
John Bawdon for goods	£3	18d
Henry Warddrapper for goods	100s	2s 6d
John Orchard, plumber, for goods	£4	2s
Gregory Jane for goods	40s	12d
John Nycold for goods	40s	12d
John Pytford for goods	£3 6s 8d	20d
Richard Stycke for goods	nil	
William Hole, tucker, for wages	26s 8d	4d
William Schere for goods	40s	12d
John Dayman for goods	40s	12d
Roger Peryham for goods	100s	2s 6d
Stephen Grene for wages	20s	4d
John Newland for wages	nil	
Roger Weldow for wages	20s	4d
William Mounstevyn for wages	20s	4d
John Cheryte for wages	20s	4d
Robert Shawe, tailor, for wages	20s	4d
John Mounstephyn for wages	£20	20s
Thomas [blank] for wages	20s	4d
Beatrix William, widow, for goods	£20	20s
John Hurston for goods	100s	2s 6d
John Oldom for goods	100s	2s 6d
Richard Vyncent for wages	20s	4d
Thomas Marke for wages	20s	4d
John Ley for goods	4 marks	16d
John Wyotte, weaver, for wages	20s	4d
Charles [blank] for goods	40s	12d
Richard Toker for wages	20s	4d
Richard Glover for wages	20s	4d
Thomas Dawe for wages	20s	4d
William Percy for goods	4 marks	16d
John Voysey, tailor, for wages	20s	4d
William Tompson for goods	5 marks	20d
Thomas H. . . for wages	20s	4d
Thomas Whyte for goods[1]	£10	5s
. . . for wages	20s	4d
. . . Salter, cook, for goods	£3	18d
Thomas Arundel for goods	£16	8s
. . ., his servant, for wages	20s	4d
James Lar. . . for goods	40s	12d
Nicholas Pawlett for goods	£4	2s
Roger . . . for wages	20s	4d
John . . . for goods	100s	2s 6d
Thomas Hilyng for goods	£10	5s
. . ., his servant, for wages	26s 8d	4d
. . .orth for goods	£10	5s
. . . for goods	40s	12d
. . . for wages	20s	4d
. . . for goods	10 marks	3s 4d
. . . for wages	20s	4d
. . . for goods	40s	12d
. . . for goods	£100	£5
. . . for wages	20s	4d
. . . for goods	100s	. . .
. . .	20s	4d
. . .	20s	4d
. . . for wages	20s	4d
. . . for goods	20s	4d
. . . for wages	20s	4d
. . . for wages	20s	4d
. . . for goods	40s	. . .
. . . for goods	40s	12d
. . . for wages	26s 8d	4d
. . . for goods	£10	5s
. . .	£6	6s
. . .lyn for wages	40s	. . .
. . . for wages	20s	8d
. . . for wages	20s	4d
. . . for goods	40s	12d
John . . . for goods	£6	3s
John . . . for wages	20s	4d
Thomas . . .ale for wages	20s	4d
. . . for wages	20s	4d
. . . glover for wages	20s	4d
Margery Notte, widow, for wages	20s	4d
Margaret Menhale for wages	20s	4d
John Prynce for wages	20s	4d
Richard D. . . for goods	40s	12d

Total £16 14s 6d

1 See Appendix I.

THE SUBSIDY OF 1544

[Abstract of Heading] Indenture made 20 November 36 Henry VIII [1544] between Thomas Prestwode, mayor of the city of Exeter, Thomas Denys, knt., John Harrys, esq., sergeant-at-law, William Hurst and William Peryham, Commissioners of the King in the matter of the second payment of the subsidy granted by Parliament 35 Henry VIII whereby they nominate John Midwynter and Robert Midwynter, both of Exeter, merchants, chief collectors to receive and levy of Richard Sweyt and Henry Maunder, citizens and merchants, as much as appears below, to the use of the King.

Thomas Prestwoode	mayor	John Harrys
Thomas Denys		William Hurst

PARISH OF HOLY TRINITY

John Wolcott, gent., for lands	£20	20s	
Thomas Elysworthy for goods	£3	3d	
John Sabytt, inhabitant, for goods	40s	4d	
John Pyman for goods	40s	2d	
Richard Stubbys for goods	£5	10d	
John Stevyns for goods	£13	4s 4d	
Richard Turney for goods	£5	10d	
Nicholas Walrond for goods	£26	17s 4d	
Roger Cholayshe for goods	£10	3s 4d	
Thomas Mantell for goods	20s	1d	
John Knyght for goods	40s	2d	
William Lyngham for goods	40s	2d	
Robert Alway, gent., for goods	£10	3s 4d	
John Grene for goods	£5	10d	
John Colker for goods	20s	1d	
Nicholas Chalcrasse for goods	£4	4d	
John Trystram for goods	40s	2d	
Thomasine Atwyll, widow, for lands	£5	20d	
Agnes Tuckfyld, widow, for lands	£5	20d	
Thomas Badcoke for goods	£3	3d	
John Geffrey for goods	20s	1d	
Thomas Willyames for goods	£10	3s 4d	
John Poke, inhabitant, for goods	£3	6d	
Ivan Tryssa, inhabitant, for goods	20s	2d	
John Alcoke for goods	20s	1d	
Thomas Gilbert for goods	20s	1d	
John Davy for goods	20s	1d	
Christine Thomas, widow, for goods	20s	1d	
Henry Bawthe for goods	£20	13s 4d	
Robert Glamfyld for goods	20s	1d	
Richard Blackemore for goods	20s	1d	
William Pyper for goods	20s	1d	
Gregory Jane for goods	£10	3s 4d	
John Cole for goods	40s	2d	
Roger Courtes, baker, for goods	20s	1d	
William Banyon for goods	£3	3d	
Thomas Rudgeman for goods	£3	3d	
. . . Hullond for goods	40s	2d	
. . . Tysard for goods	£6	12d	
John Marshall, smith, for goods	£6	12d	
Hugh Derham for goods	£6	12d	
John Cooke for goods	20s	1d	
John Uprysse for goods	40s	2d	
Alice Cottyn, widow, for goods	20s	1d	
John Bawdon junior for goods	£3	3d	
Rhys Dowell for goods	40s	2d	
John Bryan for goods	£5	10d	
Thomas Wyggewood for goods	20s	1d	
John Mounstevyn for goods	£40	26s 8d	
Beatrice Mounstevyn for goods	£5	10d	

Colin Petytt, inhabitant, for goods	20s	2d
Richard Bragh for goods	£4	4d
Richard Dyer for goods	20s	1d
John Bawdon senior for goods	£4	4d
John Beden for goods	40s	2d
Griffin Smyth for goods	£3	3d
Elizabeth Cooke, widow, for goods	£3	3d
Alice Wescott, widow, for goods	£3	3d
. . . Petherycke for goods	£3	3d
Thomas Derke for goods	£3	3d
Stephen Bullyn for goods	£8	16d
William Webber for goods	£10	3s 4d
John Germyn for goods	£6	12d
Richard Kettell for goods	£3	3d
William Hooper for goods	£3	3d
John Nicolles for goods	£6	12d
Alice Whyte, widow, for goods	£3	3d
John More for goods	£4	4d
John Savage for goods	£3	3d
John Oldon for goods	£5	10d
James Harrys for goods	£3	3d
Robert Davy for goods	20s	1d
Giles Mugg for goods	£3	3d
Michael Fregyn for goods	£3	3d
John Gyrse for goods	20s	1d
John Derke for lands	£11	7s 4d
Thomas Wescott for goods	£15	5s
Thomas Cause for goods	20s	1d
John Shirwell for goods	20s	1d
Total £6 15s 2d		

PARISH OF ST MARY MAJOR

Robert Toker for lands	40 marks	26s
Thomas Somerton for goods	20s	1d
Thomas Palmar for goods	20s	1d
John Davy for goods	20s	1d
John Cheryton for goods	20s	1d
John Alyn, cook, for goods	£30	20s
John Hyll for goods	£30	20s
George Bullyn for goods	£4	4d
William Bybery for goods	40s	2d
Thomas Lambert for goods	£20	13s 4d
John Symons, cook, for goods	£20	13s 4d
Laurence Asterlegh for goods	20s	1d
Henry Betty for goods	£6	12d
Richard Undey for goods	40s	2d

Walter Wymont for goods	20s	1d
Lambert Johnson, inhabitant, for goods	£10	6s 8d
Robert Chesterton, for goods	£3	3d
William Marchaunt, inhabitant, for goods	20s	2d
Robert Toker, hosier, for goods	£3	3d
James Sueth, inhabitant, for goods	£5	20d
Robert Gregory for goods	20s	1d
Thomas Nicolles for goods	£6	12d
Thomasine Humfrey, widow, for goods	20s	1d
John Welshe for goods	£3	3d
William Rycrost for goods	40s	2d
George Burnell for goods	£4	4d
Thomas Fydavy for goods	20s	1d
James Loye for goods	20s	1d
Richard Moggryge for goods	40s	2d
John Rysdon for goods	£3	3d
Tristram Warton for goods	5 marks	3d
Nicholas Bonamye for goods	40s	2d
Margery Carrowe, widow, for goods	40s	2d
Alice Brydgeman, widow, for goods	£15	5s
Edward Brydgman for goods	£9	18d
Richard Wylcockes for goods	£14	4s 8d
John Style for goods	20s	1d
Walter Trott for goods	£12	4s
Tristram Weston for goods	20s	1d
John Wylcokys at Palys for lands	£5	20d
Alice Robynatt, widow, for goods	20s	1d
Anthony Master, alien		1d
John Aparys, alien		1d
Wilmot Cottyn, widow, for goods	£8	16d
Margaret Taylor, widow, for goods	£6	12d
Edmund Gye for goods	40s	2d
Henry Clarke for goods	20s	1d
James Clyff for goods	40s	2d
Francis Barnehowse, alien, for goods	20s	2d
Thomas Cheyney for lands	20s	2d
Richard Yong for goods	£4	4d
Henry Savage for goods	40s	2d
John Cornyshe for goods	20s	1d

John Stowell for goods	£20	13s 4d		Ralph Paty for goods	40s	2d
John Richardys for goods	20s	1d		John Gilbert for goods	40s	2d
Gest Garrett, alien, for goods	£6	2s		William Pereson for goods	20s	1d
John Shae for goods	40s	2d		John Welseman for goods	20s	1d
Isabrant Crenye, alien for goods	20s	2d		John Way for goods	20s	1d
John Walter for goods	20s	1d		Thomas Martyn for goods	20s	1d
John Wyllys for goods	40s	2d		Avis Horwyll for goods	20s	1d
Michael Browne, alien, for goods	£8	2s 8d		Thomas Moy for goods	20s	1d
Walter Randell for goods	£3	3d		William Typson for goods	20s	1d
Thomas House for goods	£8	16d		Nicholas Wall for goods	20s	1d
John Jackeson for goods	40s	2d		Peter Baker for goods	£5	10d
Robert Edmundes for goods	40s	2d		John Jew for goods	20s	1d
Christopher Mayre for goods	20s	1d		Johane Crear for goods	20s	1d
William Dawston for goods	40s	2d		John Wekes for goods	20s	1d
Robert Brydgeman for goods	£5	10d		John Hutston for goods	20s	1d
John Rypley for goods	£40	26s 8d		John Langford for goods	20s	1d
William Halsse for goods	£20	13s 4d		John Coty, alien		1d
Robert Johnson for goods	£4	4d		Thomas Cady for goods	20s	1d
Sextyn Alyn for goods	20s	1d		Humphrey Voysey for goods	20s	1d
John Hamlyn for goods	20s	1d		John Taylor for goods	20s	1d
William Stevyns for goods	20s	1d		John Jamys for goods	20s	1d
William Lott for goods	£20	13s 4d		William Glamfyld for goods	£3	3d
Hugh Selett for goods	20s	1d		Tristram Glampfyld for goods	20s	1d
Cornyshe Magent for goods	20s	1d		William Barlow for goods	20s	1d
John Plympton for goods	20s	1d		Thomas Cookes for goods	£3	3d
Giles Horwyll, alien		1d		John Moy for goods	20s	1d
John Meryfyld for goods	20s	1d		William Wickett for goods	20s	1d
William Keysell for goods	20s	1d		John Hooker for lands	£14	9s 4d
Robert Harman for goods	20s	1d		Arthur Fountayne for goods	40s	2d
Edward Harman for goods	40s	2d		William Jaccobe for goods	40s	2d
John Fursdon for goods	£4	4d		Stephen Doddys for goods	20s	1d
Thomas Hanson for goods	40s	2d		Wardens of the said parish church in lands	£4	16d
Simon Fulderton for goods	20s	1d		John . . .low for goods	40s	2d
Thomas Sharke for goods	£3	3d		James Bostocke for goods	40s	2d
Augustine Knyght for goods	20s	1d		Richard Bryttell for goods	40s	2d
John Kethe for goods	£8	16d		Jasper Suest for goods	20s	1d
John Soyll for goods	20s	1d		Robert Bryant for goods	20s	1d
John Whyte for goods	20s	1d		Edward Lawley for goods	20s	1d
Elia Potter for goods	20s	1d				
John Sharke for goods	£10	3s 4d				
John Organ for goods	40s	2d				
John Shaplebotham for goods	20s	1d				
Richard Wolston for woods	20s	1d				
William Blacke for goods	40s	2d				
John Taylour for goods	20s	1d				
Simon Casemore for goods	40s	2d				
Martin Phelyppe, alien, for goods	£5	20d				

Total £11 7s 9d

PARISH OF ST GEORGE

Henry Hamlyn for goods	£60	40s
William Webb for goods	£50	33s 4d
John Thomas for goods	£40	26s 8d
Nicholas Denson for goods	40s	2d
William Hussey for goods	£10	3s 4d
Richard T . . . yng for goods	£6	12d
Richard Mutton for goods	20s	1d
William Raynoldes for goods	£30	20s

Richard Baron for goods	20s	1d	Peter Carpynter for			
Thomas Hancoke for			goods		20s	1d
goods	20s	1d	Christine Polglasse for			
William Church for			goods		20s	1d
goods	20s	1d	Richard Courtenall for			
Agnes Hengyscott, widow,			goods		20s	1d
for goods	£25	16s 8d	John Hulyn, alien, for			
John Alyn, cooke,			goods		20s	2d
junior for goods	£5	10d	Wardens of the said			
John Clevehanger for			parish church for lands	£4	16d	
goods	£15	5s	Total 10s 11d			
John Moynes for goods	£10	3s 4d				
John Pryour for goods	20s	1d				
John Carpynter for goods	40s	2d	PARISH OF ALL HALLOWS			
John Harper for goods	20s	1d	ON THE WALLS			
John Paule for goods	£30	20s	John Preston for goods	£15	5s	
Nicholas Buckeram for			Walter Gaydon for			
goods	20s	1d	goods	£15	5s	
Henry Gall for goods	40s	2d	Robert Coblond for			
John Geell for goods	20s	1d	goods	£10	3s 4d	
Balthasar Delalow, alien,			William Comyng for			
for goods	40s	4d	goods		20s	1d
Stephen Eston for goods	20s	1d	Alice Sprusse for goods		20s	1d
John Fayremax for goods	20s	1d	Geoffrey Peers for goods		20s	1d
William More for goods	20s	1d	James Carter for goods		40s	2d
Nicholas Gervys for goods	40s	2d	Thomas Hydon for goods		20s	1d
Anthony Cholayshe for			William Harvy, cooper, for			
goods	20s	1d	goods		20s	1d
Hugh Browne for goods	£10	3s 4d	Oliver Dugard, alien,			
Richard Veller for goods	£40	26s 8d	for goods		40s	4d
William Beryman for			Elizabeth Hunt, widow,			
goods	£66 13s 4d	44s	for goods		20s	1d
Robert Freer for goods	£60	40s	Thomas Byshope for			
John Gybbys for goods	20s	1d	goods		20s	1d
William Nicholys for			William Stone for goods		20s	1d
goods	20s	1d	Richard Wyll for goods	£3	3d	
Nicholas Reve for goods	£60	40s	Richard Fayreman for			
Robert Newall, alien, for			goods		40s	2d
goods	40s	4d	Christopher Burton for			
Ralph Hooper for goods	20s	1d	goods		20s	1d
Peter Pyne for goods	20s	1d	Laurence Porter for			
Thomas Cornyshe for			goods		40s	2d
goods	20s	1d	Thomas Bere for goods		20s	1d
Henry Skarche for goods	40s	2d	William Carter for			
Total £16 7s 1d			goods		20s	1d
			Philip Langaller for			
			goods		20s	1d
			Robert Derycke for			
PARISH OF ST MARY STEPS			goods		20s	1d
James Bury for goods	£10	3s 4d	Total 15s 6d			
James Taylour for goods	£13	4s 4d				
Robert Davy for goods	40s	2d				
John Skobyll for goods	40s	2d	PARISH OF ST JOHN			
Robert Northeway for			Laurence Prouz, esq., for			
goods	40s	2d	lands	£42	42s	
Alice Martyn for goods	40s	2d	William Burdon, gent., for			
Christine Thaccher,			lands	£8	2s 8d	
widow, for goods	40s	2d	Richard Jefford for			
John Coockes for goods	20s	1d	goods	£20	13s 4d	
Adrian Peter for goods	20s	1d	John Vyncent for goods	£10	3s 4d	
William Gybbys for goods	20s	1d	John Carpynter, alien,			
Thomas Olyver for goods	£3	3d	for goods	£20	20s	
Charles Rogers for goods	40s	2d				

Warnard Haydon, alien, for goods	£4	8d
Thomas Gryott for goods	40s	2d
Thomas Beare for goods	£5	10d
John Garlond for goods	40s	2d
Agnes Hargast, widow, for goods	£6	12d
Robert Chaff for goods	£10	3s 4d
William Lamb for goods	40s	2d
John Cobaton for goods	£5	10d
Richard Martyn, hellier, for goods	£5	10d
William Pearson for goods	£4	4d
William Smycke for goods	£4	4d
Andrew Aysheryge for goods	40s	2d
Derek Goff, alien, for goods	40s	4d
Nicholas Bennett for goods	20s	1d
Thomas More for goods	20s	1d
Jest Ray, alien, for goods	20s	2d
Roger Raynysby for goods	40s	2d
Simon Jane for goods	40s	2d
Roger Sym for goods	40s	2d
Thomas Bury for goods	40s	2d
Thomasine Prescott, widow, for goods	20s	1d
Johane Hyllyng, widow, for goods	20s	1d
Richard Farwell for goods	£4	4d
Matthew Coffyn for goods	20s	1d
Richard Jane for goods	20s	1d
William Secke for goods	20s	1d
John Spenser for goods	20s	1d
Philip Rychard for goods	40s	2d
Richard Welisdon for goods	20s	1d
William Jefford for goods	20s	1d
Magdalena Dyer for goods	20s	1d
Philip Mannyng for goods	40s	2d
Philip Dawe for goods	20s	1d
John Sage for goods	20s	1d
Henry Herrell for goods	20s	1d
Thomas Marshall for goods	£20	13s 4d
Nicholas Hooper for goods	20s	1d
John Lane, butcher, for goods	40s	2d
Agnes Greston for goods	20s	1d
John Gilbert for goods	20s	1d
John Colles for goods	20s	1d
John More for goods	20s	1d
John May for goods	£5	10d
Henry Marshall for goods	£13	4s 4d

John Howell for goods	£6	12d
Wardens of the Fraternity of the Blessed Mary for lands	£4	16d
Total £5 14s 7d		

PARISH OF ST OLAVE

William Peryham for goods	300 marks	£6 13s 4d
Richard Swete for goods	100 marks	44s
John Paramore for goods	£33	22s
Maurice Levermore for goods	£40	26s 8d
John Peryham for goods	100 marks	44s
Margaret Lyall, widow, for goods	£20	13s 4d
Agnes Wetherygg for goods	£10	3s 4d
William Downe for goods	£20	13s 4d
Lewis Sage for goods	£15	5s
Alice Hyll, widow, for goods	£6	12d
Milstana Whyddon, widow, for goods	£6	12d
Margaret Colton, widow, for goods	£5	10d
Edmund Colton for lands	£4	8d
William Cosyn for goods	£5	10d
John Gotley for lands	£5	20d
Richard Bery for goods	£4	4d
William Drayton for goods	£4	4d
Richard Mauncell for goods	£3	3d
John Tyrlew for goods	£4	4d
John Jane for goods	20s	1d
Johane Rede, widow, for goods	£6	12d
Laurence Edmundes for goods	20s	1d
Simon Horton for goods	£8	16d
William Shepehard	£4	4d
Nicholas Gall for goods	20s	1d
Robert Pagett for goods	£3	3d
Luke Seynt John for goods	20s	1d
John Skarborough for goods	£3	3d
Peter Sayer for goods	40s	2d
Robert Drayton for goods	£4	4d
Winifred Whyddon for goods	40s	2d
Cornelius Hay, alien, for goods	20s	2d
John Amery for goods	40s	2d
Edmund Deane for goods	£20	13s 4d
John Stranger, alien		1d
Thomas Huchyns for goods	£20	13s 4d

William Underhay for goods	20s	1d
Robert Dene for goods	20s	1d
John Toker for goods	40s	2d
Thomas Balhachett for goods	40s	2d
William Morrys, plumber, for goods	40s	2d
Nicholas Seyward for goods	£3	3d
William Apryse for goods	20s	1d
Total £17 4s 6d		

PARISH OF ST MARY ARCHES

John Trubody for goods	£10	3s 4d
John Hurst for goods	£40	26s 8d
Robert Cotton for goods	£30	20s
John Grenefyld, esq., for lands	£80	£4
John Blackealler for goods	100 marks	44s
Gilbert Kyrke for goods	£160	£5 6s 8d
John Way for goods	£50	33s 4d
John Maynerd for goods	£60	40s
John Crast for goods	£20	13s 4d
Bernard Gould for goods	£60	40s
Juliana Smyth, widow, for goods	£10	3s 4d
Richard Mawdytt for goods	£20	13s 4d
Humphrey Androw for goods	£25	16s 8d
William Gomby for goods	£20	13s 4d
Henry Maunder for goods	£30	20s
William Morrys for goods	£15	5s
Nicholas Banckes, tailor, for goods	£10	3s 4d
Robert Hayward for goods	£4	4d
John Huwett for goods	£20	13s 4d
William Poyntyll for goods	£20	13s 4d
John Burnell for goods	£4	4d
Edith Carter, widow, for goods	£5	10d
Richard Way for goods	£15	5s
Nicholas Maunder for goods	£3	3d
Thomas Grene for goods	£20	13s 4d
John Dumpayne for goods	£5	10d
Yowham Garrett, alien, for goods	40s	4d
Johane Rawlyn, widow, for goods	20s	1d
Elizabeth More for goods	20s	1d
George Hullond for goods	£7	14d
John Androwe for goods	£5	10d
Christopher Blackealler for goods	40s	2d
John Maynerd junior for goods	£10	3s 4d

Robert Colston for goods	40s	2d
John Wynsham for goods	20s	1d
Wardens of the said parish church for lands	40s	8d
Total £26 16s 10d		

PARISH OF ST PETROCK

William Hurst for goods	400 marks £8 17s 4d	
John Brycknall for goods	£200 £6 13s 4d	
Thomas Hunt for goods	£200 £6 13s 4d	
William Bucknam for goods	200 marks £4 8s 8d	
John Buller for goods	200 marks £4 8s 8d	
John Drake for goods	£100	66s 8d
John Mydwynter for goods	200 marks £4 8s 8d	
William Smyth for goods	100 marks	44s
Christopher Potter for goods	£40	26s 8d
Griffin Amaredyth for lands	£40	40s
John Massy for goods	£30	20s
Philip May for goods	£30	20s
William Person for goods	£20	13s 4d
John Wolcott, merchant, for goods	£30	20s
William Seldon for goods	£20	13s 4d
John Robyns for goods	£9	18d
William Whyte for goods	£10	3s 4d
Robert Hunt for goods	£20	13s 4d
Gilbert Saywell for goods	£8	16d
Johane Chanons, widow, for goods	£9	18d
Richard Maynerd for goods	£40	26s 8d
John More for goods	£5	10d
John Wyggmore for goods	£4	4d
Alexander Trygges for goods	£5	10d
Robert Bostocke for goods	£7	14d
John Langher for goods	£4	4d
John Cheryton for goods	£3	3d
John Mutton for goods	40s	2d
Avis Hynckes, widow, for goods	£5	10d
Richard Hynckes for goods	£5	10d
William Tuckefyld for goods	40s	2d
John Engleton for goods	40s	2d
Robert Boell for goods	40s	2d
Tristram Carrow for goods	20s	1d
Stephen Parker for goods	40s	2d
Robert Butler for goods	40s	2d
Peter Stracche for goods	£5	10d

Henry Bystetor, alien,
for goods | £4 | 8d
John Nicolles, alien,
for goods | 20s | 2d
Paul Stafford for goods | £30 | 20s
Roger Hawker for goods | £13 | 4s 4d
Johane Germyng for
goods | £5 | 10d
Peter Lake for goods | £5 | 10d
Simon Shute for goods | 40s | 2d
Hugh Sentlehay for goods | £9 | 18d
Wardens of the said parish
church for lands | £6 | 4s
Total £53 18d

PARISH OF ST MARTIN

Thomas Spurway for
goods | £100 | £3 6s 8d
Thomas Collyns for goods | 20s | 1d
John Tuckefyld for
goods | £100 | £3 6s 8d
John Shalys for goods | 40s | 2d
William Tothyll for goods | £60 | 40s
Nicholas Lymett for
goods | £80 | 53s 4d
Thomas Skydmore for
goods | £20 | 13s 4d
Thomas Spyser for goods | £20 | 13s 4d
John Toker for goods | £20 | 13s 4d
William Davy for goods | £10 | 3s 4d
Charles Southern, for
goods | £16 | 5s 4d
John Burgeys for
goods | 20 marks | 4s 4d
Thomas Myghell for
goods | 20s | 1d
Robert Dyrham for goods | £10 | 3s 4d
John Paunchard for
goods | 20s | 1d
John Gamon for goods | 20s | 1d
John Wall for goods | 40s | 2d
John Woodbeare for
goods | 40s | 2d
William Collyns for goods | 40s | 2d
Johane Halsse for goods | 20s | 1d
John Browne for goods | 40s | 2d
John Bury for goods | £60 | 40s
John Waut for goods | 20s | 1d
John Alsope for goods | 20s | 1d
Walter Newcomb for goods | 20s | 1d
Thomas Smyth for goods | £3 | 3d
John Smyth for goods | £40 | 26s 8d
John Hall for goods | £16 | 5s 4d
William Phelyppe for
goods | 20s | 1d
Julian Morrys, alien,
for goods | £10 | 6s 8d
Francis Obyn, alien | | 1d
John Parr for goods | £20 | 13s 4d
John Broke, alien, for
goods | 40s | 4d

Robert Farnell for goods | £3 | 3d
John Rawlyn for goods | 20s | 1d
Richard Martyn for
goods | 20s | 1d
John Dayman for goods | £40 | 26s 8d
John Sheller for goods | £30 | 30s
Henry Mocke for goods | £16 | 5s 4d
Johane Drayton for
goods | 20s | 1d
Richard Smarte for
goods | £16 | 5s 4d
Richard Bartelett for
goods | 40s | 2d
Roger Hall for goods | 20s | 1d
John Kethe junior for
goods | 20s | 1d
Oliver Manneryng for
goods | £30 | 20s
George Manneryng for
goods | £5 | 10d
William Burne for
goods | 20 marks | 4s 4d
Richard Wyllyams for
goods | £6 | 12d
Thomas Honychurch for
goods | 40s | 2d
Walter Hext for goods | 20s | 1d
Thomas More for goods | 20s | 1d
Richard Pendy for goods | 20s | 1d
Thomas Jonys for goods | 20s | 1d
Adam Clarke for goods | 20s | 1d
William Cruse, gent.,
for goods | £3 | 3d
Robert Seyntlon for goods | 20s | 1d
William Lentall for goods | 20s | 1d
William Cooke for goods | 20s | 1d
. . . Welles for goods | 20s | 1d
Christopher Kyrrycke for
goods | 20s | 1d
Nicholas Amore for
goods | 20s | 1d
Thomas Morrys for
goods | 20s | 1d
Robert Levys for goods | 20s | 1d
Thomas Jacobb for
goods | 40s | 2d
Thomas Coll for goods | 20s | 1d
Edmund Old for goods | 40s | 2d
Gilbert Booke for goods | 20s | 1d
John Welsheman for goods | 20s | 1d
William Butler for goods | 20s | 1d
Anthony Colman for
goods | 20s | 1d
Thomas Cole for goods | 20s | 1d
John Shurte for goods | 40s | 2d
Thomas Rede for goods | 20s | 1d
William Martyn for
goods | 20s | 1d
Richard Whyddon for
goods | 20s | 1d
Roger Pery for goods | 20s | 1d
John Cryspyn for goods | 20s | 1d

Two pinners, with John
Cryspyn, clerk, for their
goods   £4   4d
  Total £23 14s 10d

PARISH OF ST STEPHEN

John Holmer senior for goods	£40	26s 8d
Elizabeth Kyrkeham, widow, for lands	£20	20s
Roger Wallys for goods	£20	13s 4d
Thomas Chapell for goods	£15	5s
William Huchyns for goods	£12	4s
Agnes Hole, widow, for goods	£10	3s 4d
Gilbert Payge for goods	£10	3s 4d
Henry Toner for goods	£5	10d
John Raynysby for goods	£5	10d
Elizabeth Barnehowse for lands	£5	20d
Matthew Cobley for goods	£3	3d
John Heache, alien, for goods	£5	20d
Stephen Heryng for goods	40s	2d
Hugh Twechyn for goods	40s	2d
Richard Paunsford, for goods	40s	2d
John Lugar Johnson, alien	20s	2d
Thomas Ballard for goods	40s	2d
Thomas Ryder for goods	£3	3d
Richard Fowke for goods	£3	3d
William Symons for goods	40s	2d
Henry Marshall, merchant, for goods	20s	1d
Robert Trowe for goods	40s	2d
Edward Classe for goods	£5	10d
Roger Trederff for goods	40s	2d
Alexander Torker for goods	40s	2d
John Whyte for goods	20s	1d
Richard Prestwood for goods	£7	14d
Peter Venderbake, alien	40s	4d
Osmund Willyams for goods	40s	2d
Roger Robynson for goods	40s	2d
Maurice Yrysman for goods	40s	2d
John Appryse for goods	20s	1d
George Johnson for goods	40s	2d
Baldwin Toker for goods	20s	1d
James Evystys for goods	40s	2d
John Holmer junior for goods	£7	14d
Thomas Prestwode for goods	£180	£6
Total £10 7s 7d		

PARISH OF ST LAWRENCE

William Gybbys, esq., for lands	£10	6s 8d
John Anthony for lands	£10	6s 8d
Richard Wallys for goods	20s	1d
Robert Horwood for goods	£18	6s
John Parker for goods	20s	2d
John Hyll for goods	40s	2d
Thomas Smyth for goods	20s	1d
Nicholas Banckes, cutler, for goods	40s	2d
Richard Hert for goods	£15	5s
Richard Hunt for goods	£15	5s
William Petty for goods	£15	5s
John Lymbery for goods	£15	5s
William Hert for goods	£5	10d
William Luppyngcott for goods	£26	17s 4d
Elizabeth Larder, widow, for lands	20 marks	8s 8d
Hugh Ward for goods	20s	1d
John Blateyove, alien, for goods	40s	4d
William Weer for goods	20s	1d
Lewis Pollard for lands	£5	20d
Robert Bromefyld for goods	40s	2d
Robert Hephow for goods	20s	1d
John Tylly for goods	20s	1d
John Paunchard for goods	20s	1d
John Osteler for goods	20s	1d
John Brend for goods	40s	2d
Elia Gay for goods	20s	1d
Michael Phelyppe for goods	20s	1d
John Shulder for goods	20s	1d
Edward Carwythan, gent., for goods	£20	13s 4d
Thomas Hurr for goods	20s	1d
Nicholas Karselake for goods	20s	1d
Richard Horwyll for goods	40s	2d
Philip Howe for goods	£15	5s
Thomas Bale for goods	20s	1d
John Helman for goods	£15	5s
John Pardys for goods	£3	3d
Roland Robynson for goods	40s	2d
William Grygg for goods	£15	5s
John More for goods	40s	2d
John Brogyn for goods	40s	2d
John Downey for goods	£9	18d
Hugh Cardynam for goods	20s	1d
William Gybbys for goods	20s	1d
Wardens of the Fraternity of the chapel of the Holy Trinity for lands	40s	8d
Total £5 21d		

PARISH OF ALL HALLOWS GOLDSMITH STREET

Richard Hert, gent., for goods	£30	20s
Edward Seywell for lands	£8	2s 8d
Nicholas Rough for goods	£20	13s 4d
Peter Lapkyn, alien, for goods		1d
William Hawe for goods	£10	3s 4d
John Saunder for goods	20s	1d
William Balhacchett for goods	20s	1d
James Brend, alien, for goods	£3	6d
Gregory Hayward for goods	£3	3d
John Bodlegh for goods	£50	33s 4d
Sandy Napper, alien, for goods	£10	6s 8d
Thomas Stevyns for goods	20s	1d
William Peryman for goods	20s	1d
Thomas Richardson for goods	£6	12d
Nicholas Quashe for goods	20s	1d
John Lane for goods	£10	3s 4d
William Woodcocke for goods	£3	3d
William Knellys for goods	20s	1d
John Hooper for goods	£4	4d
Stephen Vylvayne for goods	£40	26s 8d
John Colford for goods	20s	1d
Peter Engleton for goods	£5	10d
John Northbroke for lands	£20	20s
Thomas Walker for goods	20s	1d
Robert Vaughan for goods	£5	10d
John Glasse for goods	20s	1d
Thomas Hampton for goods	20s	1d
William Hundaller for goods	20s	1d
Barnard Johnson, alien, for goods	20s	2d
John Harrys for goods	£5	10d
Thomas Peter for goods	£5	10d
John Gropall, alien, for goods	£10	6s 8d
Elizabeth Germyng for goods	20 marks	4s 4d
Edward Russell for goods	£8	16d
William Lant for goods	20s	1d
Peter Trose, inhabitant, for goods	£20	20s
Richard Colwyll for goods	£60	40s
Total £10 8s 7d		

PARISH OF ST PAUL

William Beannit, gent., for goods	£6	12d
Richard Martyn for goods	40s	2d
Thomas Davy for goods	40s	2d
William Moylys for goods	20s	1d
William Larkebere for goods	20s	1d
Johane Polglasse for goods	20s	1d
Johane Martyn for goods	40s	2d
Robert Thomas for goods	20s	1d
William Hunt for goods	£5	10d
Alice Cuckbender for goods	20s	1d
John Helyer for goods	40s	2d
Wardens of the Fraternity of Tailors for goods	£14	9s 4d
Alice Barnard for goods	£3	3d
Johane Ryse for goods	20s	1d
Thomas Trevell for goods	£3	3d
John Ogyn for goods	20s	1d
Thomas Tawny for goods	20s	1d
John Hayne for goods	20s	1d
John Lake for goods	£20	13s 4d
John Bell for goods	20s	1d
John Hutton for goods	£3	3d
Thomas Meryfyld for lands	£5	20d
Nicholas Furnere for goods	20s	1d
John Sondyford for goods	£5	10d
William Selman for goods	40s	2d
John Phelyppe, smith, for goods	£8	16d
William Downeman for goods	£40	26s 8d
Thomas Jesse for goods	40s	2d
William Austyn for goods	20s	1d
Thomas Thacher for goods	£33	22s
John Thaccher for goods	20s	1d
Stephen Smyth for goods	£10	3s 4d
Total £4 3s 2d		

PARISH OF ST PANCRAS

Richard Ratclyff for goods	£100	£3 6s 8d
Richard Lymbery for goods	£40	26s 8d
Henry Harrys for goods	£50	33s 4d
Richard Toker for goods	40s	2d
Thomas Befyzt for goods	£30	20s
John Blackealler for goods	£30	20s
William Cottyn for goods	£25	16s 8d
William Aysheborne for goods	£30	20s
Richard Harrys for goods	£3	3d
Geoffrey Parr for goods	£10	3s 4d

Edward Cruse for goods	£10	3s 4d
John Jonys for goods	£8	16d
Thomas Daw for goods	£8	16d
John Treby for goods	£6	12d
Walter Martyn for goods	£4	4d
John Toker for goods	40s	2d
Edmund Rough for goods in the custody of Richard Ratclyff	£8	16d
Pinners [sic] of Richard Ratclyff for their goods from the legacy of a certain Thomas Mitchell, clerk, lately deceased	£40	26s 8d

Total £12 2s 7d

PARISH OF ST KERRIAN

Richard Denys, gent., for goods	£20	20s
John Androw for goods	20s	1d
Hugh Pope for goods	£40	26s 8d
Nicholas Lyta, alien, for goods	40s	4d
William Burgeys for goods	£20	13s 4d
John Martyn for goods	20s	1d
Robert Mydwynter for goods	£30	20s
Thomas Grygg for goods	£33	22s
Thomas Zely for goods	20s	1d
John Freer for goods	20s	1d
John Drew for goods	£10	3s 4d
John Dyxston for goods	£8	16d
John Molbyn for goods	20s	1d
George Brewton for goods	£10	3s 4d
Nicholas Smote for goods	40s	2d
Mary Potter, widow, for lands	£5	20d
Elizabeth Marrys, widow, for goods	£20	13s 4d
Agnes Marche, widow, for goods	20 marks	4s 4d
John Chase for goods	20s	1d
Johane Pery, widow, for goods	£10	3s 4d
Eleanor Horton, widow, for goods	£4	4d
Godfrey Harman, alien, for goods	£8	2s 8d
Stephen Nannyng, alien, for goods	£10	6s 8d
John Gellett, alien, for goods	£3	6d
William Wylkyns for goods	40s	2d
Richard Hawkys for goods	40s	2d
Peter Seby for goods	40s	2d
Wardens of the said parish for lands	22s	4d

Total £7 4s 8d

PARISH OF ST DAVID

John Payne for goods	20s	1d
John Myddelton for goods	£5	10d
William Pycketon for lands	40s	4d
John Sampford for goods	£4	4d
Elizebeth Appryse for goods	20s	1d
John Morrys for goods	20s	1d
Nicholas Stansyll for goods	20s	1d
Humphrey Petty for goods	20s	1d
John Cotyford for goods	£5	10d
Johane Shere widow for goods	20s	1d
Walter Walter for goods	20s	1d
Thomas Ratclyff for goods	£10	3s 4d
Henry Comb for goods	20s	1d
William Oplond for goods	£4	4d
Mabel Roche, widow, for goods	20s	1d
Johane Lyneham for goods	20s	1d
Margery Raglond for goods	20s	1d
John Valans for goods	£19	6s 4d
John Aysheton for goods	40s	2d
Laurence Yowland for goods	20s	1d
Robert Marryner for goods	40s	2d
John Cooper for goods	20s	1d
Henry Hayman for goods	20s	1d
Stephen Kenford for goods	20s	1d
Laurence Crosseman for goods	20s	1d
William Jeffrey for goods	20s	1d
John Roo for goods	£6	12d
William Cooper for goods	£10	3s 4d
John Myldon for goods	£5	10d
Peter Venycomb for goods	20s	1d
Richard Hullond for goods	20s	1d
Richard Bygnard for goods	20s	1d
Richard Wallys for goods	£5	10d
Robert Roo for goods	£6	12d
John Gore for goods	£12	4s
William Marrys, clerk, for lands	20s	2d
Roger Redlake, clerk, for lands	20s	2d
Roger Valland for goods	40s	2d
Roger Halstaff for goods	20s	1d
John Newland for goods	20s	1d

Total 26s

Total of all parishes aforesaid £213 3s

THE SUBSIDY OF 1557/8

[m.1a] John Peter mayre

Thomas Prestwoode
John Mydwynter

PARISH OF HOLY TRINITY

Robert Frye, gent., for lands	£10	40s
Anthony Lawe for goods	£5	13s 4d
Robert Brute for goods	£5	13s 4d
Matthew Drake for goods	£5	13s 4d
Gregory Jane for goods	£5	13s 4d
John Stevens for goods	£5	13s 4d
William Bryckenall for goods	£5	13s 4d
John Bryantt for goods	£12	32s
John Jerman for goods	£5	13s 4d
Robert Edmondes for goods	£5	13s 4d
Total [blank]		

PARISH OF ST MARY MAJOR

John Hyll for goods	£10	26s 8d
Thomas Lambert for goods	£12	32s
William Trevytt for goods	£8	21s 4d
Lambert Johnson for goods	£6	37s 4d
Robert Toker for goods	£5	13s 4d
Philip Drever for goods	£6	16s
Richard Moggrydge for goods	£5	13s 4d
Edward Brydgeman for goods	£13 6s 9d	35s 7d
John Shorte for goods	£8	21s 4d
John Bedycomb for goods	£5	13s 4d
Peter Colton for goods	£10	26s 8d
John Repley for goods	£40	106s 8d
William Toker for lands	£4	16s
Thomas Howse for goods	£10	26s 8d
Michael Browne, alien, for goods	£8	42s 8d
James Garrett, alien, for goods	£15	£4
Ralph Duckynfyld for goods	£20	53s 4d
John Hucker for lands	£5	20s
William Payke for goods	£5	13s 4d
John Cottey, alien, for goods	£3	16s
[m.1b] Martin Philyppes, alien, for goods	£4	21s 4d

John Gilyes for goods	£5	13s 4d
William Rhytt, alien, for goods	20s	5s 4d
Geoffrey Thomas for goods	£10	26s 8d
William Hulytt for goods	£5	13s 4d
John Redward for goods	£5	13s 4d
Thomas Warde for goods	£7	18s 8d
Elinor Sharke, widow, for goods	£8	21s 4d
Peter Baker for goods	£5	13s 4d
William Frye for goods	£5	13s 4d
Margery Carew, widow, for lands	20s	4s
Mary Baggwyll for goods	£5	13s 4d
Lewis Lusters, alien, servant with Martin Phylyppes		8d
John Dewlond, alien, servant with the same Martin		8d
Richard Philyppes, alien, servant with the same Martin		8d
James Wyght, servant, with Nicholas Bonamey		8d
Wardens of this parish for lands belonging to the said church	40s	8s
Total [blank]		

PARISH OF ST GEORGE

Richard Prowse for goods	£8	21s 4d
Philip Cane for goods	£5	13s 4d
Thomas Johnson for goods	£5	13s 4d
Richard Helyer for goods	£6	16s
John Baker for goods	£6	16s
Richard Gervys for goods	£5	13s 4d
Elizeus Ratclyff for goods	£5	13s 4d
Simon Herton for goods	£10	26s 8d
John Powle for goods	£9	24s
Thomas Bevys for goods	£5	13s 4d
William Clarke for goods	£5	13s 4d
Beatrix Freer, widow, for goods	£5	13s 4d
Nicholas Reve for goods	£20	53s 4d

Thomas Perkyn for
goods　　　　　　£6　　　16s
James Shere, alien, for
goods　　　　　　£3　　　16s
Cornelius Hayes, alien,
for goods　　　　　20s　　5s 4d
　　　Total [blank]

PARISH OF ST EDMUND

Michael Hastynges for
goods　　　　　　£5　　13s 4d
Humphrey Wynde for
goods　　　　　　£5　　13s 4d
William Denys for goods　£6　　16s
[Nicholas in a later hand]
Wescott, widow for
lands　　　　　　£5　　　20s
Thomas Dyer for goods　£5　　13s 4d
Richard Wyllys for
goods　　　　£13 6s 9d　35s 7d
Richard Burdon for
goods　　　　　　£10　26s 8d
William Geffrey for
goods　　　　　　£5　　13s 4d
John the Bryttyn, alien　　　　8d
Wardens of that church for
the lands belonging to the
said church　　　　£3　　　12s
　　　Total [blank]

PARISH OF ALL HALLOWS ON THE WALLS

John Jamez for goods　£5　　13s 4d
Isebrand Grene, alien,
for goods　　　　　　　　　8d
Warnard Haydon, alien　　　　8d
Oliver Degarde, alien　　　　8d
　　　Total [blank]

[m.2a] PARISH OF ST JOHN
Richard Gyfforde for
goods　　　　£35 £4 13s 4d
John Howell for goods　£10　26s 8d
Richard Taylor, brewer,
for goods　　　　　£10　26s 8d
Richard Taylor, *tucker*,
for goods　　　　　£9　　24s
John May for goods　　£5　　13s 4d
John Carpynter, alien, for
goods　　　　　　30s　　8s
Josse, alien, for goods　　　　8d
Wardens of the Fullers
and Weavers for their
lands　　　　　　40s　　8s
　　　Total [blank]

PARISH OF ST MARY ARCHES

John Peter, mayor, for
goods　　　　£80 £10 13s 4d
John Parker, esq., warden,
for his lands　　20 marks　53s 4d
John Blackealler for
goods　　　　£13 6s 9d　35s 7d
Robert Mydwynter for
goods　　　　　　£30　　£4
John Crwldey [*sic*] for
goods　　　　£13 6s 9d　35s 7d
Rose Way, widow, for
goods　　　　　　£8　　21s 4d
Henry Maunder for
goods　　　　　　£11　29s 4d
Robert Chaff for goods　£15　　40s
Robert Cotten for goods　£6　　16s
John Antony for goods　£7　18s 8d
Edward Lymytt for goods　£10　26s 8d
Alexander Cryges for
goods　　　　　　£12　　32s
John Barstabell for goods　£6　　16s
Richard Mawdytt for
goods　　　　　　£8　　21s 4d
Elizabeth Comb, widow,
for goods　　　　　£5　　13s 4d
Edward Whytcomb for
goods　　　　　　£11　29s 4d
Andrew Gere for goods　£8　　21s 4d
George Peryman for
goods　　　　£13 6s 9d　　35s
William Gregory for
goods　　　　　　£7　18s 4d
John Wekez for goods　£8　　21s 4d
Wardens of the said
church for lands
belonging to the said
church　　　　　30s　　6d
　　　Total [blank]

PARISH OF ST OLAVE

John Greynfyld for
lands　　　　£26 8s 4d　£5 6s 8d
Maurice Levermore for
goods　　　　　£40　£5 6s 8d
John Peryem for goods　£40　£5 6s 8d
Richard Swete for goods　£20　53s 4d
John Paramore for goods　£12　　32s
William Shepherd for
goods　　　　　　£9　　24s
Richard Selwode for
goods　　　　　　£15　　40s
Henry Paramore for
lands　　　　　　20s　　4s
John Toker for goods　£5　　13s 4d
Robert Dreyton for goods　£7　18s 8d
William Nicholas for
goods　　　　　　£5　　13s 4d
John Hucchyns for
goods　　　　　　£5　　13s 4d

John Clyff for goods   £5   13s 4d
Alice Aleyn, widow, for goods   £5   13s 4d
Robert Herewarde, alien, for goods   20s   5s 4d
Philip . . .rd for goods   £5   13s 4d
Total [blank]

[m.2b] PARISH OF ST PETROCK
William Hurst for lands   £100   £20
John Mydwynter for goods   £40   £5 6s 8d
John Buller senior for goods   £40   £5 6s 8d
William Buckenam for goods   £80   £10 13s 4d
John Blackealler for goods   £40   £5 6s 8d
William Way for goods   £25   £3 6s 8d
William Seldon for goods   £25   66s 8d
William Chapell for goods   £18   48s
Eustace Olyver for goods   £10   26s 8d
Simon Knyght for goods   £17   45s 4d
Gilbert Saywell for goods   £6   16s
Robert Huntt for goods   £12   32s
Hugh Sowthey for goods   £5   13s 4d
John Bodley for goods   £5   13s 4d
Margaret Drake, widow, for goods   £30   £4
Agnes Smythe, widow, for goods   £20   53s 4d
Johane Ameredethe, widow, for goods   £5   13s 4d
John Castell for lands   £5   20s
Robert Bostocke for goods   £5   13s 4d
William Warde for goods   £5   13s 4d
John Jelys, *Baccheler*, for goods   £5   13s 4d
John Nicholas, alien   8d
Wardens of this parish for lands belonging to the said church   £4   16s
Total [blank]

PARISH OF ST MARTIN
Walter Stapelhyll for lands   £20   £4
Edward Souche for lands   £20   £4
Oliver Manarynge for goods   £20   53s 4d
Johane Tuckefylde, widow, for goods   £20   53s 4d
Thomas Marshall for goods   £13   34s 8d
James Walter for goods   £12   32s
John Bodley for lands   40s   8s

Elizabeth Totthyll, widow, for goods   £10   26s 8d
Grace Lymytt, widow, for goods   £10   26s 8d
Katherine Skydmore for goods   £8   21s 4d
Charles Sowthron for goods   £10   26s 8d
Robert Vaughan for goods   £8   21s 4d
John Daymontt for goods   £8   21s 4d
Richard Hockely for goods   £8   21s 4d
John Kychell for goods   £6   16s
Roger Robynson for goods   £5   13s 4d
Robert Geer for goods   £5   13s 4d
Richard Smert for goods   £6   16s
John Smythe for goods   £14   37s 4d
Thomas Spycer for goods   £12   32s
John Toker for goods   £6   16s
Juliana Morrys   8d
Francis, servant of Julian Skynner   8d
Total [blank]

[m.3a] PARISH OF ST STEPHEN
Thomas Prestwoode for lands   £60   £12
Richard Prestwoode for goods   £15   40s
Thomas Rychardson for goods   £10   26s 8d
Thomas Chapell for goods   £8   21s 4d
John Webbe for goods   £8   21s 4d
Richard Hasellwoode for goods   £10   26s 8d
John Reynsby for goods   £5   13s 4d
Thomas Smythe for lands   20s   4s
John Hacche, alien, for goods   £4   21s 4d
Peter Sanderbecke, alien   8d
Bernard Harryson, alien, for goods   20s   5s 4d
Nicholas Wyllyams, alien   8d
James Pyke, alien   8d
Total [blank]

PARISH OF ST LAWRENCE
Johane Carew, widow, for lands   £6   24s
Robert Horwoode for goods   £13 6s 9d   35s 7d
William Lyppencote for goods   £5   13s 4d

William Grygge for
goods   £8   21s 4d
William Gater for goods   £7   18s 8d
Michael Jerman for
goods   £10   26s 8d
William Pettye for goods   £7   18s 8d
Richard Huntt for
goods   £6   16s
Johane Bery, widow,
for goods   £10   26s 8d
John Prygges for goods   £5   13s 4d
Richard Wallys for
goods   £5   13s 4d
Robert Laverye for lands   40s   8d
John Pardyse for goods   £5   13s 4d
Total [blank]

PARISH OF ALL HALLOWS GOLDSMITH STREET

Richard Hert for goods   £18   48s
Hubert Colwyll for
goods   £6   16s
John Northbroke for
goods   £20   53s 4d
William Lante for goods   £7   18s 8d
Elizabell Gale, widow,
for goods   £6   16s
Peter Trose, alien,
for goods   £12   £3 4s
Henry Robertes for
goods   £6   16s
Thomas Peter for
goods   £5   13s 4d
Stephen Vylvayne for
goods   £18   48s
Ambrose Torr, alien,
for goods   £4   21s 4d
Thomas Bearde for goods   £7   18s 8d
Sandy Napper, alien,
for goods   £15   £4
Arnold Reynoldes, alien,
for goods   £4   21s 4d
Nicholas Row for goods   £17   45s 4d
Yougham Garratt, alien   8d
Peter Lapkyn, alien   8d
Francis Lavandale, alien   8d
Gilbert Tayler, alien,
servant of Henry Robertes   8d
Nicholas Huberts, alien,
servant of Stephen
Vylvayne   8d
Robert Martin, alien,
servant of Alexander
Naper'   8d
Laurence Mathew, alien,
servant of Arnold
Reynoldes   8d
John Quinte, alien,
servant of Hugh Symons   8d
Total [blank]

[m.3b]   PARISH OF ST PAUL
John Wyllsby for lands   £20   £6
William Downeman for
goods   £10   26s 8d
Thomas Berdsyld for
goods   £5   13s 4d
Robert Bartres, alien,
servant of Geraint
Bowhay   8d
Total [blank]

PARISH OF ST PANCRAS

Henry Harrys for goods   £20   53s 4d
Henry Wolcote for
goods   £10   26s 8d
John Jerman for goods   £5   13s 4d
John Paz for goods   £9   24s
William Hunt for goods   £8   21s 4d
William Cotten for goods   £10   26s 8d
Jago Rayle, alien   8d
Total [blank]

PARISH OF ST KERRIAN

Marion Denys for lands   £10   40s
Thomas Grygge for goods   £30   £4
John Dyer for goods   £20   53s 4d
Peter Lake for goods   £20   53s 4d
Robert Way for lands   40s   8d
Hugh Pope for goods   £30   . . .
John Wolcote for
goods   £13 6s 9d   35s 7d
Stephen Nannynge, alien,
for goods   £5   26s 8d
Martin Barbynson, alien,
for goods   £5   26s 8d
Gilbert Harman, alien,
for goods   £7   xxx . . .
John Blayttyce, alien   8d
Arnold Betmaker, alien   8d
John Gilberte, alien,
servant of Martin
Barbynson   8d
Total [blank]

PARISH OF ST SIDWELL

William Woodcocke for
lands   40s   8s
Richard Mylbury for
goods   £5   13s 4d
Robert Peryam for lands   40s   8s
John Saturley for goods   £5   13s 4d
Christopher Comysherd,
pro feodis suis   40s   8s
Hugh Davy for goods   £5   13s 4d
Simon Carew for lands   40s   8s
Edmund Halstaff for
goods   £5   13s 4d
Gregory Sawyer for
goods   £5   13s 4d

William Snell for lands	40s	8d
John Hoper for goods	£5	13s 4d
Roger Johns for goods	£6	16s
William Clover for		
goods	£6 13s 2d	17s 9½d
William Slocomb for		
goods	£5	13s 4d
John Downehay for		
goods	£5	13s 4d
William Pycton for lands	40s	8s
Peter Harrys, *Baccheler*, for		
goods	£5	13s 4d
Thomas Russell for		
goods	£5	13s 4d

[m.4a] PARISH OF ST MARY STEPS

Christine Bryckenall for		
goods	£10	26s 8d
John Bonyfaunt for		
goods	£8	21s 4d
John Burne for goods	£6	16s
Johane Taylor for goods	£5	13s 4d
William Challys for		
goods	£5	13s 4d
Juliana Norton for goods	£5	13s 4d
John Englyshe, alien		8d

James Taylor for		
goods	£6 13s 2d	17s 9½d
Ambrose Howell for		
goods	£5	13s 4d
Wardens of this parish for		
lands belonging to the		
said church	£3	12s
Total [blank]		

PARISH OF ST DAVID

Thomas Geffrey for		
goods	£5	13s 4d
Roger Wallans for goods	£7	18s 8d
William Coper for goods	£5	13s 4d
Johane Drew for goods	£5	13s 4d
Thomas Twege for		
goods	£5	13s 4d
Robert Row for goods	£9	24s
Thomas Ratclyff for		
goods	£10	26s 8d
Michael Hobbye, alien,		
servant of Robert Rowe		8d
David Gander for goods	£5	13s 4d
Total [blank]		
Sum Total [blank]		

THE SUBSIDY OF 1577

[Abstract of Heading] Indenture made 14 September 19 Elizabeth [1577] between William, bishop of Exeter, Robert Chaffe, mayor, . . ., Thomas Southcott, John Blackaller, William Peryam, . . . Bruerton, esq., the Queen's Commissioners for the levying and collection of the second payment of a subsidy levied on lands and tenements in the said city on the one part, and John Vowell *alias* Hooker of the said city, gent., and Edward Herte of the same city, gent., on the other part, whereby it is witnessed that the Commissioners appoint John Vowell *alias* Howker and Edward Herte to be the chief collectors.

Robert Chaffe mayor

Wy Peryhm

Thomas Southcote

Thomas Bruarton

PARISH OF ST MARY MAJOR					
William Trevett in goods	£16	[16s]	Thomas Hampton in goods		. . .
Laurence Seldon in goods	£5	5s	William Tooker, gent., in lands		. . .
John Watkins in goods	£3	3s	Nicholas Carpenter in goods		. . .
William Mungwell in goods	£6	6s	Robert Midwinter in goods		. . .
Laurence Bonefilde in goods	£3	3s	Richard Bowdon in lands		. . .
Thomas Baskervile in goods	£3	3s	Laurence Serell in goods		. . .
Richard Rowe in goods	£5	5s	William Peake in goods		. . .
Richard Gifforde in goods	£10	10s	Richard Stansbye in goods		. . .
Laurence Barcombe in goods	£6	6s	John Tothell, gent., in goods		. . .
Anthony Thomas in goods	£3	. . .	William Dodridge in goods		. . .
William Rawley, esq., in lands	£20	. . .	Michael Bridgman in lands		. . .
John Peeke in goods	£4	. . .	John Blackaller in lands		. . .
Andrew Hill in goods	£3	. . .	John Geane in goods		. . .
John Yeo, gent., in goods	£5	. . .	John Shere in goods	£5	. . .
William Martyn in goods	£4	. . .	Thomas Odam in goods	£6	. . .
John Shorte in goods	£6	. . .	Richard Sirante in goods	£5	. . .
John Hawkerudge in goods	£5	. . .	[m.1b] Roger Mace in goods	£3	
William Piggons in goods	£5	. . .	Thomas Shorte in goods	£4	
Robert Edmondes in goods	£3	. . .	Margaret Poole, widow, in lands	20s	
John Hooker, gent., in lands	£5	. . .	William Grenewoode in lands	20s	
Ralph Keate, gent., in goods	. . .		Miles Lamberte in goods	£3	
Feet Lendon, alien, in lands	. . .		*Straungers*		
			John Gilberte, alien, Francis Foynate	4d	
			John, servant of Walter Hunte	4d	
			Total . . .		

61

PARISH OF ALL HALLOWS
[ON THE WALLS]
John Stansbye in goods
Richard Miller in goods
Edward Williams in
goods

Total 9s

PARISH OF ALL HALLOWS
GOLDSMITH STREET
William Parker, gent.,
in lands   £13 6s 8d
Alexander Napper, alien,
in goods   £7   ...
Ambrose Torr, alien,
in goods   £4   ...
Peter Trosse, alien,
in goods   £6   ...
Edward Herte
in goods   £6   ...
John Pill in goods   £10   ...
Peter Vilvaine in
goods   £5   ...
John Dorr in goods   £3   3s
Hubert Collwill in
goods   £3   3s
Agnes Erle, widow, in
lands   20s   16d

Total £4 1d

PARISH OF ST MARY STEPS
John Bonifante in goods   £4   4s
Thomas Martyn in goods   £4   4s
Christine Bricknall, widow,
in goods   £5   5s
Henry Dabinot in goods   £3   3s
Andrew Mawrye in
goods   £3   3s
Gregory Hunte in goods   £3   3s
Elizabeth Bourne in
goods   £3   3s
Nicholas Moore in goods   £3   3s
John Berye in goods   £3   3s
Edward Waglande in
goods   £3   3s

Total 34s

PARISH OF ST GEORGE
Richard Hellier in
goods   £8   8s
Mary Castell, widow,
in goods   £3   3s
Alexander Mayne in
goods   £8   8s
William Budgell in goods   £6   6s
William Perye in goods   £3   3s
Nicholas Spicer in goods   £8   8s
Clement Owlborrowe
in goods   £3   3s

Peter Harris in goods   £3   3s
[m.2a] William Buckforde in
goods   £10   10s
William Garrett in goods   £5   5s
John Gifforde in goods   £3   3s
John Ellarde in goods   £3   3s
Richard Darnell in goods   £3   3s
Thomas Harris in goods   £3   3s
Richard Erle in goods   £3   ...
Philip Somerton in
goods   £3   3s
John Pawle in goods   £3   3s
Richard Gervis in goods   £3   3s
Digory Baker in lands   20s   16d
William Paine in goods   £3   3s
Francis Brina, alien, in
goods   £6   12s

Total £4 17s 4d

PARISH OF ST PANCRAS
Richard Prouze in lands   £10   13s 4d
Laurence Radforde in
lands   £10   13s 4d
William Hunte in goods   £6   6s
John Challis in lands   20s   16d
John Brooks in goods   £3   3s
Philip Yearde in goods   £8   8s
Thomas Richardes in
goods   £5   5s
William Webbe in goods   £3   3s

Total 53s

PARISH OF ST MARTIN
Thomas Southcott, esq.,
in lands   £40   53s 4d
William Peryam, esq.,
in lands   £20   26s 8d
Thomas Bruerton
goods   £20   20s
John Smithe in goods   £16   16s
Elizabeth Tothill,
widow, in goods   £5   5s
Hugh Wyott, gent.,
in lands   £3   ...
John Weston, gent., in
goods   £10   10s
Walter Jones in goods   £6   6s
Henry Southeron in
goods   £6   6s
Gilbert Staplehill in
goods   ...   3s
Robert Michell in goods   £3   3s
Edmund Grene in goods   £3   3s
John Dyer in goods   £5   5s
Christopher Mannaringe
in goods   £3   3s
Richard Bartlett in
lands   20s   15...
William Masters in
goods   £3   ...

Nicholas Wyott in goods	£3	. . .
Thomas Trosse in goods	£4	. . .
William Bruton in goods		. . .
Christopher Spicer in		
goods		. . .
John Howell in goods		. . .
John Averye junior in		
goods		
Richard Juell in goods		
Richard Newman in		
goods		
Thomas Spicer in goods		
Peter Willis in lands		
Nicholas Bolt in goods		

Total £11 10s 8d

PARISH OF ST OLAVE

William Hurste esq.,		
in lands		. . .
John Pery . . .		
John Br . . .		
[m.2b] William She . . .		
Alice Sweete in goods		. . .
John Chapell in goods		. . .
Valentine Tooker in		
goods		. . .
Thomas Chaffe in goods	£3	
John Fallett in goods		. . .
Richard Dorchester in		
goods		. . .
John Tozer in goods		. . .
Maurice Downe in		
goods		. . .
Margery Vilvaine,		
widow, in goods		. . .
Jeremy Garrett in goods		. . .
Thomas Poinctingdon in		
goods		. . .
John Hutchins in goods		. . .
John Collins in goods		. . .

Total v . . . ij[s] iiijd

PARISH OF ST JOHN

John Howell in goods	£8	8s
Robert Chaffe junior in		
goods	£3	3s
John Applyn in goods	£5	5s
William Flea in goods	£3	3s
Thomas Marshall in		
goods	£30	30s
Thomas Berie in goods	£3	3s
Nicholas Eron in goods	£8	8s
George Dodridge in		
goods	£3	3s
Edward Warde in goods	£3	3s
James Torrington in		
goods	£3	3s
The Corporation of Weavers		
and Tuckers in lands	£3	. . .

Emmanuel Tailour in		
goods	£3	3s
Margaret Mericke, widow,		
in goods	£6	6s
Thomas Marshall for that		
which the same did not		
account before the said		
Commissioners on the		
day fixed for the		
taxation of the		
said subsidy according		
to the Act and subsidy	40s[1]	

Total £6 2s

PARISH OF ST PAUL

Michael Jurden in goods	£5	5s
John Buggins in goods	£5	5s
Thomas Jurden in goods	£3	3s
John Downe in goods	£4	4s
John Trewman in goods	£3	3s
Richard Edmondes in		
goods	£4	4s

Total 24s

PARISH OF ST EDMUND

William Holder in goods	£5	5s
George Reve in goods	£5	5s
John Partrudge in goods	£3	3s
William Wilkins in goods	£3	3s
Richard Pittes in lands	20s	16d
Richard Meane in goods	£3	3s
Robert Tremell in goods	£3	3s
Richard Willes in goods	£10	10s
William Heywoode in goods	£4	4s

Total 37s 4d

PARISH OF ST PETROCK

Robert Chaff, mayor, in		
goods	£20	20s
John Blackall' in lands	£14	18s
William Chapell in		
goods	£30	30s
Simon Knight in lands	£20	26s . . .
[m.3a] Nicholas Martyn in		
goods	£30	30s
Henry Ellacott in goods	£16	16s
John Jones in goods	£14	14s
John Webbe in goods	£16	16s
William Martyn in		
goods	£20	20s
John Levermore in goods	£12	12s
Eustace Oliver in goods	£12	12s
Hugh Wilston in goods	£16	16s
George Smithe in goods	£20	20s
Thomas Chapell in goods	£12	12s
Richard Herdinge in		
goods	£10	10s
Thomas Heathe in goods	£10	10s

[1] *Received 11 January aforesaid 40s by the hand of William Marshall son of the said Thomas*, in margin,

John Tooker, merchant		
in goods	£6	6s
Robert Webber in goods	£10	10s
John Feilde in goods	£6	6s
Richard Maye in goods	£4	4s
John Trosse in goods	£3	3s
Henry Ellis in goods	£3	3s
Thomas Ellis in goods	£3	3s
Christopher Weste in		
goods	£3	3s
Richard Perrie in goods	£3	3s
Henry Paine in goods	£3	3s
Margaret Hunte, widow,		
in goods	£5	5s
Lawrencia Seldon, widow,		
in goods	£3	3s
Pascacia Budley, widow,		
in goods	£3	3s
John Nicholles, alien		4d
John Spurwaie in goods	£3	3s
Thomas Bridgeman in		
goods	£3	3s
George Prestwood,		
gent., in lands	£10	13s 4d
Total £17 18s		

PARISH OF ST KERRIAN

George Peryamn in goods	£20	20s
Anthony Halstaffe in goods	£3	3s
Robert Waie in lands	£4	5s 4d
Henry Hull in goods	£4	4s
John Sandye in goods	£4	4s
Thomas Turbervile in		
goods	£6	6s
John Redwoode in goods	£3	3s
Peter Benson in goods	£3	3s
Edward Coaks in goods	£3	3s
Godfrey Harmon, alien,		
in goods	£4	8s
Francis Tooker in goods	£3	3s
Robert Dyer in goods	£3	3s
Richard Sweete in goods	£6	6s
John Sampforde in		
goods	£6	6s
Total £3 17s 4d		

PARISH OF ST STEPHEN

Henry Clevelande in
goods
Richard Paunsforde in goods
Nicholas Hatche in goods
Thomas Raymonde in lands
Henry James in goods
Richard Beckingham in
goods

Total 41s 4d

PARISH OF HOLY TRINITY

Robert Frye, gent., in		
lands	£3	. . .

Peter Wolcott in lands	£5	
Henry Waller in lands	£3	
[m.3b] Geoffrey Thomas		
in goods	£12	
John Moore in goods	£5	
Michael Frigon in		
goods	£3	
Ciprian Neele in goods		
William Paine in goods		
Philip Reynolles in goods		
Silvester Weste in goods		
Richard Christopher in		
goods		
William German in goods		
George . . .mdeitt in		
goods		
John . . .		
William . . .		
Thomas Nicholles in		
goods		
Total . . . 9s . . .		

PARISH OF ST MARY ARCHES

John Peter in lands	£30	40s
William Gibbes in goods	£20	20s
Agnes Pope, widow, in		
goods	£3	3s
John Anthonye in goods	£8	8s
Brice Hill in goods	£5	5s
Johane Blackaller in		
goods	£6	6s
Thomas Midwinter in		
goods	£5	5s
John Dodd in goods	£5	5s
Andrew Geare in lands	20s	12d
John Hackwell in goods	£5	5s
Richard Bevis in goods	£5	5s
John Bastable in goods	£3	3s
William Phillippes in		
goods	£3	3s
Richard Maudett in		
lands	20s	16d
Elizabeth Levermore, widow,		
in goods	£3	3s
Thomas Martyn in goods	£20	20s
John Davie in goods	£16	. . .
Total £7 9s 8d		

PARISH OF ST LAWRENCE

Richard Denys, esq., in		
goods	£10	10s
Humphrey Carewe, gent.,		
in lands	40s	2s 8d
Michael German in goods	£16	16s
William Grigg in goods	£15	15s
Grace Birde, widow,		
in goods	£3	3s
Philip Biggelstone in		
goods	£6	6s

Mary Herte, widow,			Edward Chicke in lands	20s	16d
in goods	£5	5s	John Furnys in goods	£3	3s
Richard Pettie in goods	£5	5s	William Slocombe in		
John Wethycombe in			goods	£3	3s
goods	£3	3s	Roger Chardon in goods	£3	3s
John Serell in lands	40s	2s 8d	John Tooker, brewer,		
William Russell in			in goods	£3	3s
goods	£3	3s	Richard Bicknall in goods	£3	3s
Thomas Manning in			Martin Bowerman in		
goods	£3	3s	goods	£3	3s
Total £3 14s 4d			Total 56s 8d		

PARISH OF ST SIDWELL

PARISH OF ST DAVID

Simon Horton in goods	£4	4s	Gilbert Denys, gent., in		
William Tooker in goods	£4	4s	goods	£6	6s
Thomas Milwarde in goods	£4	4s	Robert Rowe in goods	£10	10s
Nicholas Stockeman in			Thomas Gefferye in		
goods	£3	3s	goods	£4	4s
Nicholas Rowe in goods	£6	6s	John Skynner in goods	£4	4s
[m.4] John Gee in goods	£3	3s	Thomas Twigges in goods	£3	3s
Margaret Chardon, widow,			Nicholas Dyer in goods	£3	3s
in goods	£3	3s	Roger Valans in goods	£3	3s
John Gill in goods	£3	3s	John Cooper in goods	£3	3s
William Cover in goods	£3	3s	Bartholomew Middelton		
Johane Davie, widow,			in goods	£3	. . .
in goods	£3	3s	Total 39 . . .		
John Satterley in lands	20s	16d	Sum Total £93 13s 9d		

THE SUBSIDY OF 1586

[Abstract of Heading] Indenture made 5 September 28 Elizabeth [1586] between John, bishop of Exeter, Nicholas Martyn, mayor, Robert Denys, knt., recorder, Thomas Southcott and Thomas Bruerton, esqs., the Queen's Commissioners for the levy and collection of the second payment of a subsidy on the lands and tenements, goods and chattels levied and assigned in the city, granted to the Queen and her successors in the parliament held at Westminster 29 March 27 Elizabeth [1585], on the one part, and John Vowell *alias* Hooker of Exeter, gent., and Edward Herte of the said city, gent., of the other part, witnessing that the said Commissioners appoint John Vowell *alias* Hooker and Edward Herte to be the chief collectors of the subsidy within the city and to render account in the Exchequer.

John Exon
Nicholas Martyn mayor
Thomas Brereton

PARISH OF ST PANCRAS

Richard Prouze in lands	£10	13s 4d
John Prouze in goods	£5	5s
John Brooke in goods	£4	4s
William Skynner in goods	£3	3s
Richard Cover in goods	£3	3s
John Challis in goods	£3	3s
Edward Serle in goods	£3	3s
William Hunte in goods	£4	4s
Philip Yarde in goods	£8	8s
Total 46s 4d		

PARISH OF ST MARTIN

William Peryam, esq., one of the Queen's justices of the Court of Common Pleas, in lands	£30	40s
Thomas Southcott, esq., in lands	£50 £3	6s 8d
Thomas Bruerton, esq., in goods	£20	20s
Hugh Wiat, gent., in lands	£6	8s
John Weston, gent., in goods	£12	12s
Christopher Mawaringe, esq., in goods	£5	5s
John Dier, gent., in goods	£10	10s
Thomas Walker in goods	£12	12s

Richard Drewe in goods	£5	5s
William Bruton, gent., in goods	£12	12s
Christopher Spicer in goods	£8	8s
Richard Bertlett in lands	20s	16d
William Masters in goods	£4	4s
Thomas Trosse in goods	£7	7s
Edward Greene in goods	£3	3s
Robert Dunscomb in goods	£3	3s
John Dight in lands	20s	16d
Richard Juell in goods	£3	3s
Alan Hackwell in goods	£3	3s
Edward Locke in lands	20s	16d
William Warde in goods	£3	3s
John Ryder junior in lands	20s	16d
Richard Langhan in lands	20s	16d
Richard Collscott in lands	20s	16d
John Dynham in goods	£3	3s
Thomas Spicer in goods	£14	14s
Richard Newman in goods	£5	5s
Total £12 14s 8d		

[m.1b] PARISH OF ALL HALLOWS ON THE WALLS

John Stansebi in goods	£3	3s
Richard Miller in goods	£3	3s

William Bruer in lands	20s	16d
Elizeus Flea in goods	£4	4s
Total 11s 4d		

PARISH OF ST MARY STEPS

Thomas Martyn in goods	£6	6s
Henry Dabinet in goods	£3	3s
Andrew Mawrie in goods	£3	3s
Gregory Hunte in goods	£5	5s
Tristram Pridham in goods	£4	4s
John Rewe in goods	£3	3s
Thomas Herde in goods	£3	3s
John Aisheleigh in goods	£3	3s
John Tyrrie in goods	£3	3s
Edward Wagland in goods	£3	3s
Nicholas Evans in goods	£3	3s
John Bonifant in lands	20s	16d
Norman Morehed, alien		4d
Cornelius Foster, alien		4d
Total 41s		

PARISH OF ST SIDWELL

Robert Webber in lands	20s	16d
Edward Chicke in goods	£4	4s
Roger Chardon in goods	£4	4s
Martin Bowreman in goods	£3	3s
John Gye in goods	£3	3s
John Furnis in lands	20s	16d
John Gilberte in goods	£3	3s
Richard Bricknoll in goods	£3	3s
Robert Carowe in goods	£3	3s
George Rowe in goods	£3	3s
John Mogridge in goods	£3	3s
James Brocadon in goods	£3	3s
William Morrishe in goods	£3	3s
Robert Radford in goods	£3	3s
John Clavell in goods	£3	3s
Thomas Mannynge in goods	£3	3s
Agnes Milward, widow, in goods	£3	3s
Johane Davy, widow, in goods	£3	3s
Peter Mogridge in lands	20s	16d
William Grice in lands	20s	16d
Roger Davie in lands	20s	16d
Thomas Bricknoll in lands	20s	16d
William Alford in lands	20s	16d
John Calie in lands	20s	16d
Nicholas Stockman in goods	£3	3s
John Tooker in goods	£3	3s
William Reynolls in goods	£3	3s
William Buckford in goods	£20	20s
Total £4 9s 8d		

PARISH OF ST GEORGE

Richard Hilliard in lands	40s	2s 8d
William Garret in goods	£4	4s
Peter Harris in goods	£4	4s
Jeremy Hilliard in goods	£4	4s
William Payne in goods	£5	5s
William Perie in goods	£3	3s
Zewell Bettie in goods	£3	3s
Richard Erell in goods	£3	3s
Daniel Baker in goods	£3	3s
William Budgell in goods	£3	3s
Thomas Harris in goods	£3	3s
Alexander Mayne in goods	£8	8s
Total 45s 8d		

[m.2a] PARISH OF ST JOHN

Edward Warde in goods	£3	3s
John Howell senior in goods	£5	5s
Robert Chaffe in goods	£3	3s
Richard Reynolls in goods	£6	6s
William Pope in goods	£3	3s
William Flea in goods	£3	3s
Elizabeth Sweete, widow, in goods	£3	3s
Nicholas Dynnam in goods	£3	3s
Thomas Ackland in goods	£3	3s
Thomas Bynnam in goods	£3	3s
Corporation or society of Weavers and Fullers in lands	£3	4s
Nicholas Eron in goods	£12	12s
William Marshall in goods	£40	40s
Total £4 11s		

PARISH OF ST MARY MAJOR

Katherine Rawlie, widow, in lands	£10	13s 4d
Laurence Seldon in goods	£14	14s
John Watkins in goods	£3	3s
William Moungwell in goods	£6	6s
Richard Rowe in goods	£6	6s
Agnes Thomas, widow, in goods	£4	4s
Nicholas Bolte in goods	£3	3s
John Shorte in goods	£8	8s
John Hooker, gent., in lands	£5	6s 8d
Gilbert Smythe in goods	£7	7s
Robert Midwinter in goods	£3	3s
Thomas Edwardes in goods	£5	5s

Laurence Serle in goods	£4	4s
Richard Stansbie in lands	20s	16d
John Geane in goods	£6	6s
Simon Tailor in goods	£10	10s
Thomas Odam in goods	£6	6s
Margaret Pole, widow, in lands	20s	16d
William Greenewood in goods	£3	3s
Thomas Grenewood in goods	£8	8s
John Paine in goods	£8	8s
Thomas Baskervile in goods	£6	6s
John Dipford in goods	£5	5s
Richard Maddicke in goods	£4	4s
Richard Bodye in goods	£4	4s
Walter Cowse in lands	20s	16d
Walter Bodye in goods	£4	4s
John Anthonye in lands	20s	16d
Humphrey Gilberte in goods	£3	3s
Christopher Battyn in lands	20s	16d
William Martyn in goods	£3	3s
William Rede in lands	20s	16d
Richard Sergente in lands	20s	16d
Thomas Hampton in goods	£10	10s
Laurence Barcomb in goods	£10	10s
Nicholas Carpenter in goods	£7	7s
Total £9 8s		

PARISH OF ST LAWRENCE

Humphrey Carewe in lands	40s	2s 8d
Michael Germyn in goods	[erased] li	
Philip Biggilston in goods	£10	10s
Walter Denys in lands	£3	4s
Mary Herte, widow, in goods	£5	5s
John Germyn in lands	£5	6s 8d
John Vylveyne in goods	£4	4s
John Serell in goods	£5	5s
Michael Smoote in lands	40s	2s 8d
William Russell in goods	£4	4s
Richard Barons in goods	£3	3s
Hugh Sampford in lands	40s	2s 8d
Anthony Piggott in goods	£3	3s
Agnes Dowtey, widow, in goods	£3	3s
Richard Liell in goods	£3	3s
William Grigge in goods	£10	10s
Alexander Germyn in goods	£7	7s
Total £4 10s 8d		

[m.2b] PARISH OF ALL HALLOWS GOLDSMITH STREET

William Parker, esq., in lands	£13 6s 8d	17s 9½d
John Pill in goods	£10	10s
Edward Herte, gent., in goods	£8	8s
William Germyn in goods	£4	4s
Peter Vylveyne in goods	£6	6s
Agnes Torr, widow, in goods	£3	3s
John Averie in goods	£3	3s
William Newcomb in goods	£3	3s
Michael Colwill in lands	40s	2s 8d
Thomas Banckes in lands	20s	16d
John Garret in lands	20s	16d
John Elliott in lands	20s	16d
Humphrey Baker in lands	20s	16d
Total £3 2s 9½d		

PARISH OF ST OLAVE

William Hurste, esq., in lands	£30	40s
John Periam in goods	£16	16s
John Collins in goods	£6	6s
William Shepperde in goods	£3	3s
John Brushford in goods	£6	6s
William Brailey in goods	£7	7s
Richard Dorchester in goods	£5	5s
John Radford in goods	£6	6s
John Tozer in goods	£4	4s
Thomas Chaffe in goods	£5	5s
Eleanor Horsey, widow, in lands	20s	16d
Paul Trigges in goods	£3	3s
Thomas Pointingdon in goods	£3	3s
John Maynerd in lands	20s	16d
Robert Bennet in goods	£4	4s
Hugh Bidwell in goods	£3	3s
Richard Thatcher in goods	£3	3s
John Follett in goods	£7	7s
George Drake in goods	£3	3s
Thomas Chappell in goods	£15	15s
John Chappell in goods	£12	12s
Total £7 13s 8d		

PARISH OF ST STEPHEN

George Smyth in lands	£30	40s
Henry Clevelande in goods	£8	8s
Robert Michell in goods	£7	7s

Jasper Bridgeman in lands	£8	10s 8d
John Trosse in goods	£7	7s
Clement Owleborowe in goods	£5	5s
Thomas S^tclere in goods	£3	3s
John Wythecomb in goods	£4	4s
Nicholas Hatche in goods	£3	3s
John Pitforde in goods	£3	3s
Peter Risedon in goods	£3	3s
John Younge in goods	£3	3s
Thomas Tirrie in goods	£3	3s

Total £4 19s 8d

PARISH OF ST MARY ARCHES

John Davye in goods	£20	20s
Thomas Martyn in goods	£20	20s
George Peryman in goods	£17	17s
Nicholas Spicer in goods	£16	16s
Matthew Sutcliffe, doctor of laws, in goods	£8	8s
John Hackwell in lands	£5	6s 8d
Richard Jurden in goods	£8	8s
Richard Mawditt in goods	£6	6s
John Dodd in goods	£6	6s
Agnes Pope, widow, in goods	£3	3s
Thomas Midwinter in goods	£4	4s
John Morrishe in goods	£4	4s
Robert Sherwood in goods	£3	3s
Jasper Horsey in goods	£4	4s
John Triggs in lands	20s	16d
Christopher Easton in lands	20s	16d
Richard Bevis in goods	£6	6s
John Aplyn in goods	£6	6s
Brisa Hill, widow, in lands	20s	16d

Total £7 20d

[m.3a] PARISH OF ST KERRIAN

Henry Hull in goods	£10	10s
[blank] Halstaff, widow, in lands	£3	4s
Robert Waye in lands	£4	5s 4d
Edward Langibu in goods	£8	8s
Doctor Veale, alien, in lands		4d
Thomas Turbervile in goods	£5	5s
Johane Redwoode, widow, in goods	£3	3s

Godfrey Harmon, alien, in goods	£3	6s
Thomas Chappell in lands	£10	13s 4d
Philip Prouze in goods	£3	3s
Edward Coake in goods	£4	4s
Walter Rackley in goods	£3	3s
William Weare in goods	£3	3s
John Sampford in goods	£6	6s
Richard Sweete in goods	£7	7s
Francis Dewgell, alien, in goods	£3	6s

Total £4 7s

PARISH OF HOLY TRINITY

Geoffrey Thomas in goods	£12	12s
Henry Fortescue in lands	£10	13s 4d
Robert Frye in lands	£3	4s
Peter Woolcott in lands	£4	5s 4d
George Serell in goods	£5	5s
John Blackmore in goods	£3	3s
John Lynne in lands	20s	16d
George Glubb in goods	£5	5s
Roger Edmondes in goods	£3	3s
John Moore in goods	£6	6s
Roger Selbye in goods	£6	6s
Thomas Nicolls in goods	£4	4s
John Convers in goods	£3	3s
William Payne in goods	£5	5s
Silvester Weste in goods	£4	4s
Silvester Maunder in goods	£3	3s
William Germyn in goods	£3	3s
John Rowe in goods	£3	3s
Matthew Bettie in goods	£3	3s
John Roberts, alien, in lands	20s	2s 8d

Total £4 14s 8d

PARISH OF ST PAUL

Francis Bryna, alien, in goods	£4	8s
John Downe in goods	£4	4s
Thomas Jurden in goods	£3	3s
William Hutchins in goods	£3	3s
Walter Borowe in goods	£4	4s
John Truman in lands	20s	16d
Valentine Tedberie in lands	20s	16d
Oliver Cooke in lands	£8	10s 8d
William Coomyn in goods	£4	4s
Thomas Buggins in goods	£3	3s

Total 42s 4d

PARISH OF ST EDMUND

Richard Wills in goods	£5	5s
Anthony Wyvell in goods	£4	4s
William Heywood in lands	20s	16d
Richard Pitts in lands	20s	16d
Dionisia Shere, widow, in goods	£4	4s
William Holder in lands	20s	16d
Richard Mayne in goods	£5	5s
John Deyman in goods	£5	5s
William Tyckell in goods	£3	3s
Richard Addis in goods	£3	3s
Total 33s		

PARISH OF ST DAVID

Gilbert Denys, gent., in goods	£6	6s
Richard Gyfford in goods	£10	10s
Robert Rowe in goods	£8	8s
John Skynner in goods	£5	5s
Thomas Jeffrie in goods	£4	4s
[m.3b] Thomas Twigges in lands	20s	16d
Nicholas Dier in goods	£4	4s
John Alsoppe in goods	£4	4s
William Maunder in goods	£3	3s
Richard Tillie in goods	£3	3s
John Cooper in goods	£3	3s
Robert Mogridge in goods	£3	3s
Martin Dynnam in goods	£3	3s
Robert Twiggs in lands	20s	16d
Alexander Smyth in lands	20s	16d
Robert Priggs in lands	20s	16d
Roger Valans in lands	20s	16d
John James in lands	20s	16d
Robert Downing in lands	40s	2s 8d
Thomas Pottell in lands	20s	16d
Total £3 8s		

PARISH OF ST PETROCK

Nicholas Martyn, mayor, in goods	£20	20s
John Blackall in lands	£12	16s

William Martyn in goods	£16	16s
John Howell junior in goods	£16	16s
George Prestwoode in lands	£10	13s 4d
Margaret Heath, widow, in goods	£3	3s
John Spurwaie in goods	£7	7s
Christopher Weste in goods	£5	5s
John Trosse in goods	£3	3s
Richard Perie in goods	£6	6s
Alnot Budleigh in goods	£7	7s
Alexander Baskervile in goods	£3	3s
Thomas Ellis in goods	£3	3s
Richard Chaffe in goods	£6	6s
John Ellicott in goods	£6	6s
Thomas Bridgeman in goods	£10	10s
Richard Herdinge in goods	£3	3s
John Lante in goods	£3	3s
Christine Chappell, widow, in goods	£16	16s
Elizabeth Chaffe, widow, in goods	£7	7s
Winifred Knight, widow, in lands	£10	13s 4d
Richard Wheton in goods	£5	5s
Margaret Hunte, widow, in goods	£4	4s
Hilary Galley in goods	£10	10s
Johane Ollyver, widow, in goods	£8	8s
Walter Horsey in goods	£6	6s
John Parre in goods	£4	4s
William Holmes in goods	£4	4s
William Spicer in goods	£8	8s
David Bagwell in goods	£4	4s
Henry Paine in goods	£6	6s
Nicholas Chappell in goods	£4	4s
John Nicholls, alien		4d
Henry Ellacott in goods	£16	16s
John Webbe in goods	£16	16s
John Levermore in goods	£14	14s
Total £14 12s		

Sum total £97 17½d

THE SUBSIDY OF 1593-5

PARISH OF ST PAUL

Francis Brine, alien, in goods	£5
Robert Moor in lands	£4
Oliver Coocke in lands	£4
Valentine Tedberye in goods	£4
George Leache in goods	£3
Vivian Downman in lands	£1
Humphrey Cade in lands	£1
Robert Downe in lands	£1
John Buckham in lands	£1
John Chappel junior in goods	£5
Thomas Pope in goods	£3

Jo: Chappel younger   John Davye maior
Thomas Pope   George Smythe
Tho: Denys   Richard Prouz

[p.2] PARISH OF ALL HALLOWS ON THE WALLS

William Angevyn in goods	£5
John Wills in goods	£3
Richard Miller in goods	£3
John Harrys in lands	20s
Nicholas Yeabacomb in lands	[blank]
Michael Jacob in lands	20s
Ellis Flea in goods [£3 deleted]	20s
Richard Davy in lands	40s
The Corporation of Bakers in lands	20s

John Davye maior   Rychard Prouze
Tho Denys   George Smythe

[p.3] [PARISH OF ST GEORGE]

Alexander Mane in goods	£7
William Pavie in goods	£6
Jeremy Hilliard in goods	£5
John Fishe in goods	£4
Zewell Bettey in goods	£4
Laurence Underhill in goods	£4
Peter Baker in goods	£3
William Takell in goods	£3
William Budgell in goods	£3
Daniel Baker in goods	£3
William Helmore in lands	20s
Tristram Roo in lands	20s
John Vaughan in lands	20s
Matthew German in lands	20s

John Worth in lands	20s
[John Poole in lands, 20s deleted]	
John Taile in lands	20s
[Roger Poole, 20s deleted]	
Mary Castell, widow, in lands	20s

John Davye maior   Tho Denys
Rychard Prouz   George Smythe

[p.4] PARISH OF ST DAVID

Elizabeth Dennys in goods	£6
John Skynner the elder in goods	£6
John Alsopp in goods	£6
Nicholas Dyere in goods	£5
Humphrey Holmeide in goods	£4
William Mander in goods	£4
Martin Dynnum in goods	£4
Ralph Halstaffe in goods	£3
Robert Pryges in goods	£3
Thomas Jurden in goods	£3
William Lovebone in goods	£3
Webber the Hooper in goods	£3
[Thomas Twigges in lands, 5s deleted]	
[John Coper in lands, 5s deleted]	
John Skynner in lands	20s
Roger Maye in lands	20s
Robert Downinge in lands	20s
Thomas Larramore in lands	20s

John Davye maior   Tho Denys
Rychard Prouz   George Smythe

[p.5] PARISH OF HOLY TRINITY

Mr John Wolton in goods	£10
Mr Peter Wollcote in lands	£4
Mr Norys in goods	£3
Nicholas Downe in goods	£6
Michael Thomas in lands	40s
Roger Selbye in goods	£6
John More in goods	£6
Thomas Nycolles in goods	£5
John Convers in goods	£4
Johane Forte, widow	£3
Nicholas Bolte, in goods	£4
John Blackemore in goods	£3
John Barons in goods	£3
Richard Deymaunte in goods	£3
Nicholas Wyllys in goods	£3

[Taxers in margin]

73

Edmund Modye in goods	£3
Roger Forde in lands	20s
Ralph Pawlyne in goods	£3
John Treate in goods	£3
William Mathew in goods	£3
James Bartrume in goods	£3
John Pryne, alien, in goods	£3
William Benote, alien	4d
John Davye maior	Tho Denys
Rychard Prouz	George Smythe

**[p.6]   PARISH OF ALL HALLOWS
GOLDSMITH STREET**

William Martyn, gent., in goods	£5
Edward Hert, gent., in goods	£10
William Newcombe in goods	£6
Simon de Leache in goods	£5
Nicholas Langdon in goods	£4
Thomas Banckes in lands	20s
John Ellyott in lands	20s
John Harmon in lands	20s
Thomas Jewell in lands	20s
Johane Short, widow, in lands	20s
Johane Preston in lands	20s
Henry Gandy in lands	20s
Peter Vylvayne in goods } [*Taxers*	£8
Alexander Germyn } in margin]	
in goods	£8
John Davye maior	Tho Denys
Rychard Prouz	George Smythe

[p.7]   PARISH OF ST SIDWELL

Edward Chicke in goods	£6
James Hammerton in goods	£3
Martin Bowerman in goods	£3
William Morishe in goods	£3
Nicholas Stockman in goods	£3
William Rennolls in goods	£3
Philip Pine in goods	£4
John Isacke in goods	£3
William Whitley in goods	£3
John Hoppinge in goods	£3
Robert Hewishe in goods	£3
John Cawley in goods	£3
John Pogger in goods	£3
Thomas Terrell in goods	£3
John Gilbertt in lands	20s
John Packker in lands	20s
John Mortemore in lands	20s
Thomas Robarttes in lands	20s
Richard Pyne in lands	20s
Thomas Bicknoll in lands	20s
Walter Pereym in lands	20s
[*Christopher Halstaffe in lands* 20s, deleted]	
William Gryce in goods } [*Taxers*	£3
George Rowe in goods } in margin]	£3
John Davye maior	Tho Denys
Rychard Prouz	George Smythe

[p.8]   PARISH OF ST STEPHEN

Mr George Smyth in lands	£30
Jasper Bridgeman in lands	£7
John Trosse in goods	£7
John Halstaffe in goods	£6
Johane Cleveland in goods	£4
George Periman in goods	£3
Clement Owleborow in goods	£3
Nicholas Hatche in goods	£3
Walter Cowse in goods	£3
Thomas Hamlinge in goods	£3
Thomas Wakeman in goods	£3
John Davye maior	Tho Denys
Rychard Prouz	George Smythe

[p.9]   PARISH OF ST MARY STEPS

Richard Martyn in goods	£5
Thomas Martyn in goods	£7
Thomas Herd in goods	£5
Richard Halstaffe in goods	£5
Henry Dabynet in goods	£3
John Row in goods	£3
James Taylor in goods	£3
Edward Wagland in lands	20s
Philip Geane in lands	20s
William Mortymer in lands	20s
Thomas Mayen in lands	20s
Andrew Mawry in goods	£3
Tristram Prydham in goods	£5
Norman Morehed, alien	4d
John Davye maior	Tho Denys
Rychard Prouz	George Smythe

[p.10]   [PARISH OF ST EDMUND]

Richard Mayne in goods	£5
William Holder in goods	£4
John Brewartone in goods	£4
Richard Addis in goods	£4
Zachary Wylls in goods	£3
Robert Genkeng in goods	£3
Robert Westrond in lands	20s
Thomas Ryder in lands	20s
Robert Sheare in lands	20s
William Moore in lands	20s
Robert Balle in lands	20s
Christopher Lye in lands	20s
John Davye maior	Tho Denys
Rychard Prouz	George Smythe

[p.11]   PARISH OF ST JOHN

Wyddow Marchall in goods	£8
Tuckers and Weavers in lands	£3
John Bond in goods	£3
William Mea in goods	£3
Richard Pearsson in goods	£4
William Clement in goods	£3
Robert Colls in goods	£3
William Webber in goods	£3
John Hoyell the elder in goods	£6

John Waye, schoolmaster,	
in lands	20s
Henry Taylder in lands	20s
William Tolleay in lands	20s
Willto wills in lands	20s
Emmanuel Tayldor in lands	20s
Edward Warner in goods	£5
William Pope in goods	£4
John Davye maior	Tho Denys
Rychard Prouz	

[p.12] PARISH OF ST KERRIAN

Mr Harry Hull in goods	£10
Mrs Swete, widow, in goods	£5
Richard Wheaton in goods	£5
Geoffrey Waltham in goods	£6
Giles Saverye in goods	£5
William Martyn in goods	£5
Mrs Halstaffe, widow, in lands	£3
Margaret Waye, widow, in lands	40s
Edmund Cooke in goods	£3
Philip Warde in goods	£4
John Sheare in goods	£3
Harry Osten in goods	£3
George Searell in goods	£3
Nicholas Harman in goods	£3
Philip Prowzes in goods	£3
Oliver Tappar in lands	20s
Robert Brocke in goods	£3
Mr Edward Langdon in goods	£10
Walter Borowe in goods	£6
Edward Langdon	
Walter Borowe	
John Davye maior	Tho Denys
Rychard Prouz	George Smythe

[p.13] PARISH OF ST MARY MAJOR
15th September 1595

Laurence Seldon in goods	£10
Hugh Crossing in goods	£10
Thomas Hamptone in goods	£10
Richard Gifford in goods	£10
Gilbert Smith in goods	£8
John Payne in goods	£8
John Howker, gent., in lands	£5
Thomas Edwardes in goods	£6
Richard Body in goods	£5
Hugh Morill in goods	£4
Michael Abbote in lands	20s
Henry Eliot in goods	£3
Richard Rowe in goods	£3
Edward Flude in lands	20s
Robert Hinde in goods	£4
George Drake in goods	£3
Agnes Thomas, widow, in goods	£3
Laurence Serell in goods	£5
Joan Carpenter in lands [£10 deleted]	20s
Thomas Newman in lands	20s
Thomas Keridge in goods	£3
John Taylor, innholder, in goods	£4

Simon Taylor in goods	£3
Robert Madoke in goods	£6
John Medland in lands	20s
John Garate in goods	£3
Richard Baker in goods	£3
Robert Petter in goods	£3
John Southowod in lands	20s
Mark Laverance, alien, in lands	20s
William Helliar in goods	£3
Humphrey Gilberte in goods	£3
Widow Body in goods	£4
John Diptford in goods	£5
Thomas Baskervile in goods	£5
William Lipscombe in goods	£4
William More in goods	£3
[*Widow Smarte in lands*, 20s deleted]	
Richard Retoricke in goods	£7
Robert Staphell in goods	£6
Mrs Townsend in goods	£3
Richard Reed in goods	£3
John Terry in goods	£3
Bernard Pearce in goods	£3
Laurence Barcombe in goods	£3
John Foye in goods	£3
Richard Berslye in goods	£3
John Wilmotes in goods	£3
Edward Mintron in goods	
	[in a later hand £3]
John Davye maior	Tho Denys
Rychard Prouz	George Smythe

[p.14] *The Taxacion of the Inhabitantes there for the first payment of the laste subsedy rated to her Matie in the Parliament of the xxvth yere of her highnes raigne*

PARISH OF ST MARTIN

Sir William Peryam, Knt. Lord	
Chief Baron of her Majesty's	
Court of Exchequer in lands	£45
Mr. Thomas Sowthcot, esq., in lands	£50
Hugh Wyote, esq., in lands	£6
Mr Thomas Spyser in goods	£16
Richard Dewe, gent., in goods	£3
Christopher Manwaringe, gent.,	
in goods	£5
John Bartlet, gent., in goods	£6
Christopher Spyser in goods	£13
John Rider in goods	£5
John Dynnam in goods	£5
Alan Hackwell in goods	£4
John Averye in goods	£4
William Skinner in goods	£4
Edmund Greene in goods	£3
William Warde in goods	£3
William Prowze in goods	£3
William Gardener in goods	£3
John Moggrodge in goods	£4
William Masters in goods	£5
William Ryder in goods	£3
David Hancocke in lands	20s

Richard Collescotte in lands   20s
John Lewes in lands   20s
John Pennye in lands   20s
William Weste in lands   20s
Henry Pethericke in lands   20s
John Woode in lands   20s
John Willyams in lands   20s
Christopher Hunte in lands   20s
Joseph Harrys in lands   20s
Michael Harte in lands   20s
Thomas Trose in goods   £8
Robert Parre in goods   £8
    John Davye maior   Tho Denys
    Rycherd Prouz   George Smythe

[p.15] PARISH OF ST MARY ARCHES
        22 September 1595
Mr John Davye, mayor, in lands   £20
Mr Nicholas Spiser in goods   £15
Mr Thomas Walker in goods   £14
John Hakwell in lands   £5
Robert Mychell in goods   £7
Thomas Snowe in lands   £4
Beavis Martyn in goods   £6
Paul Tryges in goods   £6
David Baggwel in goods   £6
Ignatius Jurdayn in goods   £6
Robert Sherwod in goods   £4
Alice Applen in goods   £5
John Watkenes in goods   £4
Nicholas Beves in goods   £3
John Marshall in goods   £4
John Clavell in goods   £3
John Smythe in lands   20s
Richard Beves in goods   £8
Richard Jurdayn in goods   £6
                    Total in lands £30
                    Total in goods £93
    Richard Bevis   Richard Jerdan
    John Davye maior   Tho Denys
    Rychard Prouz   George Smythe
    Jo Hele

[p.16]   PARISH OF ST OLAVE
        18th September 1595
Mr John Peryam in goods   £20
Mrs Thomasine Chapell, widow,
    in goods   £12
John Chapell in goods   £14
Richard Dorchester the elder
    in goods   £6
John Radfford in goods   £6
Thomas Chaffe in goods   £6
Thomas Poyntyngton in goods   £7
John Tayler in goods   £10
Samuel Alford in goods   £5
Christopher Eston in goods   £4
Maurice Downe in goods   £3

John Collyns the younger in goods   £3
John Wilmott in goods   £3
John Gell in goods   £3
Richard Dorchester in goods   £3
Thomas Hole in goods   £3
William Horsham in lands   20s
Nicholas Bagett in lands   20s
    [in margin viijli goods]
    John Chapell   Richard Dorchester
    John Davye maior   Tho Denys
    Jo Hele   Rychard Prouz
    George Smythe

[p.17]   The Rates to the Subsidye upon the Goodes
         and Landes of the Inhabitantes of the
         saide parish

        PARISH OF ST PETROCK
Mr. Nicholas Marten in goods   £20
Mr William Marten in goods   £16
Christine Chappell, widow, in goods   £10
Henry Payne in goods   £12
Hilary Galleye in goods   £10
Richard Chaffe in goods   £8
Alnot Budleighe in goods   £8
John Lante in goods   £8
Walter Horseye in goods   £8
John Levermoore the younger
    in goods   £6
John Marten in goods   £5
Nicholas Chappell in goods   £5
Johane Olliver, widow, in goods   £3
John Anthonye in goods [£4 deleted]   £5
John Edes in goods   £5
Richard Perrye in goods   £4
John Baker in goods   £4
Ferdinando Callender in goods   £4
John Tayler, mercer, in goods   £4
John Trosse the elder in goods   £3
Richard Brendley in goods   £3
Alexander Bascarvile in goods   £3
Thomas Blackaller in goods   £4
Robert Bennette in goods   £3
George Tayler in goods   £3
Thomas Cooke in goods   £3
Elizabeth Ellacotte, widow,
    in goods   [£7 deleted]   £8
Robert Ellacotte in goods [£6 deleted]   £7
Grace Spurway, widow, in goods   £6
Edward Clemente in goods   £3
        Rates upon Landes
Mr John Blackaller in lands   £10
John Levermoore the elder in lands   £10
Agnes Webbe, widow, in lands   £3
John Parre in lands   20s
William Tottell in lands   20s
William Wollmington in lands   20s
Thomas Withicombe in lands   20s
John Bodley in lands   20s
    The wch Rates were sett downe upon the
    said goods and Landes the xxijth daye of

September in the xxxvijth yere of the Raigne
of our Soveraigne Ladye Queene Elizabeth
Ano domini 1595 *by*
John Howell
Wyllyam Spicer
John Ellacott
Jasper Horsey
And the said Raters were themselves rated by the
Commissioners as followeth

John Howell in goods [£16 deleted]	£13
William Spicer in goods	£10
John Ellacotte in goods	£8
Jasper Horseye in goods [*in landes* deleted]	£7

John Davye maior   Tho Denys
Rychard Prouz   George Smythe

[p.18]   PARISH OF ST LAWRENCE
Mr Michael Germyn, alderman,

in goods	£10
William Buckeford in goods	£10
Jerome Alley, gent., in goods	£3
John Germyn, gent., in lands	20s
John Wotton, gent., in lands	20s
Richard Sale in lands	20s
John Wythecombe in goods	£3
Edward Esworthy in goods	£3
Philip Bigilston, *taxer*, in goods	£3
William Russell, *taxer*, in goods	£3

John Serell in goods	£3

John Davye maior   Jo Hele
Tho Denys   Richard Prouz
George Smythe
[in margin] *Mason ded*
Esworthi in his place

[p19]. *The Taxacion for the Inhabitantes of the*
parishe of St Pancras made by John
Prowze and John Sandy the xviijth
September an° 1595

Mr Richard Prowse in lands	£10
John Prowse in goods	£5
Philip Yeard in goods	£3
William Tyckell in goods	£4
Edith Hunt in goods	£3
Richard Cover in goods	£3
Thomas Richardson in goods	£3
John Challys in goods	£3
John Sandy in goods	£3
Peter Samson in goods	£3
John Tayllour in goods	£3
Total sum in lands and goods	£43

John Prowze   Tho Denys
John Sandy   John Davye maior
Jo Hele   George Smythe
Rychard Prouz

APPENDIX I

John Crugge who was assessed in the parish of St. Stephen at £500 in goods for the payment of £50 states that he paid only £12 on £240 and asks allowance of the remaining £260. He is owed £8 13s from the estate of Robert Slepe of Cornwall, decd. ' beyng nothyng worth ', £20 from John Grygge of Cornwall and £25 from Humphrey Androwe. He lost £40 out of his purse on his way to Windsor and has paid Mr. John Carewe of Bury St. Edmunds £80 for certain lands.

Richard Martyn of St. Petrock's parish assessed at 100 marks in goods for the payment of 5 marks asks an allowance of 6s 8d.

John Holmore the elder of the parish of St. Martin asks an allowance of £5.

Alice Bryggeman, widow, assessed at 200 marks in goods in the parish of St. Mary Major asks allowance of 7 marks, as she has spent £95 on the burying of her husband and the payment of his debts.

Tristram Henscott assessed at 200 marks in goods in the parish of St. George asks allowance of 33s 4d because he is owed £31 by John Coupper of London and 46s 8d by Edward Wyllowby in desperate debts.

Richard Stubbys of the parish of Holy Trinity assessed at £40 in goods for the payment of 40s asks allowance of 32s. He has paid to John Hustevater of Wells and William Summaster because he was surety for Sir Richard Wylscheir and John Come(?) the sum of £24.

John Martyn of the parish of St. Mary Steps assessed at £20 in goods for the payment of 20s asks allowance of 11s. He lost 20 marks on a loan to William Rode of Exeter, merchant, because William ' ys Fleyd '.

Thomas Whyte of the parish of Holy Trinity assessed at £20 in goods for the payment of 20s asks allowance of 15s because he has built a house which has cost him £10.

John Wolcott the younger of the parish of Holy Trinity assessed at £20 in goods for the payment of 20s asks allowance of 15s, for since the loan he paid 20 marks for the reversion of certain lands to Robert Clevehanger of Exeter.

William Hussy of the parish of St. George assessed at £200 in goods for the payment of 10 marks asks allowance of 10 marks for since the last loan ' he ys dekayed in hys Gooddes '.

Next 3 entries illegible but relate to assessments in the parishes of St. Martin, St. Petrock, and St. Mary Major.

William Hurst of the parish of St. Petrock deposed before the King's commissioners that he has lost £50 since the last loan in a ship called the *Mawdelyne* of Salcombe that was taken by Frenchmen, that he has lost by many other bad debts £40 and that he is now worth only 200 marks.

John Bala ... of the parish of St. Mary Major has lost £10 by John Tanner (?) since the last loan and by other bad debts £20 and is now worth only £10.

John Garett of the same parish has lost £8 because of sickness and bad debts since the last loan and is now worth only £18.

William Drayton of the parish of St. Olave has lost 43s since the last loan by bad debts and by the death of Christopher Prestwode and he is now worth only £18.

Thomas Hunte, baker, of the parish of St. Lawrence has lost £20 since the last loan by bad debts and he is now worth only £20.

APPENDIX II

A NOTE ON STARTING DATES OF EXETER PARISH REGISTERS

by Hugh Peskett

The parish registers of Exeter and its suburbs present considerable complexities; like many medieval cities, it was over-provided with churches, and the number has been declining since the Middle Ages. In the sixteenth century, including the cathedral, there were fifteen churches within the city walls, twenty in the City and County of Exeter, and three more in the vicinity, all keeping registers. Parish registers were ordered to start in 1538, but many of the earliest have not survived, and losses have continued into the present century, the early registers of St. Pancras having been last heard of in 1933, and those of five churches so badly damaged in the air-raids of 1942 as to be unusable. However the registers of these six parishes were transcribed by members of the Devon and Cornwall Record Society before the losses occurred. In two instances, early registers were missing in the 1830s but since have been rediscovered. Including lost originals covered by transcriptions, only three parishes, St. Mary Arches, St. Kerrian and St. Petrock, have registers starting as they should in 1538/9 (and there is some doubt whether the only two entries for 1539 in St. Kerrian's register in fact relate to that parish), two parishes just outside the city boundaries (St. Thomas 1541, Heavitree 1555) are not far behind, and eleven more start in the reign of Elizabeth. The remainder start in the second half of the seventeenth century, apart from the outer suburb of St. Leonard, which has nothing prior to 1704. However the earlier but far from complete series of bishops' transcripts antedate the registers. This level of survival compares well with that in other cities with a medieval legacy of numerous parishes, such as Bristol, Winchester, or Chichester.

Abbreviations: C—   Christenings
                 M—   Marriages
                 B—   Burials
                 BT'S— Bishops' Transcripts (mentioned only where they are the earliest original fit for production)

                 DCRS—Devon and Cornwall Record Society

Cathedral	CMB 1594
All Hallows Goldsmith Street	(C 1566, MB 1561: early volumes unfit for production but available in printed DCRS volume) originals fit for production C 1813, M 1809, B 1813 BT's from 1607
All Hallows on the Walls	C 1694, MB 1695 BT's from 1614
St. David	CMB 1559
St. Edmund	B 1571, CB 1572

81

| St. George | CMB 1682
BT's from 1609 |
| St. John | CB 1682, M 1683
BT's from 1609 |

St. George   CMB 1682
BT's from 1609

Holy Trinity   CMB 1563/4
(volume I was missing 1831, but rediscovered later)

St. John   CB 1682, M 1683
BT's from 1609

St. Kerrian   C*M 1558/9, B 1558

St. Lawrence   (CMB 1604: early volumes unfit for production, but available in DCRS copy)
BT's from 1614
originals fit for production from 1795

St. Martin   (CMB 1572: early volumes unfit for production; but available in DCRS copy)
originals fit for production C 1784, M 1754, B 1783
BT's from 1608

St. Mary Arches   CMB 1538

St. Mary Major   C 1561, MB 1562

St. Mary Steps   CMB 1655
BT's from 1610

St. Olave   C 1602, MB 1601

St. Pancras   (CMB 1664: the early volumes were lost at some time between 1933 and 1965 but the entries are available in printed DCRS volume)
originals surviving CMB 1784
BT's from 1609

St. Paul   (CMB 1562: early volumes unfit for production, but available in printed DCRS volume)
originals fit for production CB 1813 M 1754
BT's from 1609

St. Petrock   CB 1538/9 M 1539

St. Sidwell   CMB 1569

St. Stephen   (CM 1668 B[1688]: early volumes unfit for production, but available in DCRS copy)
Originals fit for production CB 1813, M 1754
BT's from 1609

*See note, supra

Parishes taken into the City of Exeter at a later date

Heavitree   C 1555, MB 1653
(baptisms register 1553–1653 was missing 1831, rediscovered later)

St. Leonard   CMB 1704
(no BT's returned before 1769 as incumbents denied the jurisdiction of the Archdeacon—without known justification)
(a burials register beginning 1610, extant in 1831, has since been lost)

St. Thomas   C 1541, M 1576/7, B 1554

KEY TO PARISHES

References are to page numbers

Parish	1489	1522	1524–5	1544	1557–8	1577	1586	1593–5
All Hallows Goldsmith Street		10	37	53	58	62	69	74
All Hallows On The Walls		—	40	48	56	62	67	73
The Close		30	—	—	—	—	—	—
Holy Trinity		22	43	45	55	64	70	73
St. David		27	41	54	59	65	71	73
St. Edmund		—	—	—	56	63	71	74
St. George	not divided into parishes	25	41	47	55	62	68	73
St. John		29	40	48	56	63	68	74
St. Kerrian		11	38	54	58	64	70	75
St. Lawrence		—	35	52	57	64	69	77
St. Martin		8	36	51	57	62	67	75
St. Mary Arches		20	39	50	56	64	70	76
St. Mary Major		14	42	46	55	61	68	75
St. Mary Steps		—	40	48	59	62	68	74
St. Olave		21	39	49	56	63	69	76
St. Pancras		9	38	53	58	62	67	77
St. Paul		13	37	53	58	63	70	73
St. Petrock		18	38	50	57	63	71	76
St. Sidwell		—	—	—	58	65	68	74
St. Stephen		7	35	52	57	64	69	74

INDEX OF PERSONS

Bokelond, Ralph, 2, 4
Bokeram see Buckeram
Bokyngham see Buckenham
Bolt (Bolte), Nicholas, 63, 68, 73
Bolter, Nicholas, 33; Roger, 7
Bonamey (Bonamye), Nicholas, 46, 55
Bond (Bonde, Bounde), Johane, 10;
John, 74; Thomas, 2, 31; —, 10
Bonefaunt (Bonefaunte, Bonifant, Boni-
fante, Bonyfant, Bonyfaunt, Bony-
faunte), John, 1, 2, 11, 14, 16, 19, 42,
59, 62, 68; Matilda, 2; Robert, 2(2);
Thomas, 14, 20, 39
Bonefilde, Laurence, 61
Boner, John, 18
Bonewyle, John, 3
Bonifant, Bonifante, Bonyfant, Bonyfaute
see Bonefaunt
Booke, Gilbert, 51
Borowe, Walter, 70, 75(2)
Bostocke, James, 47; Robert, 50, 57
Bounde see Bond
Bourchier, John, lord Fitz Warin, 14, 17,
19(2)
Bourne, Elizabeth, 62
Bowdon (Bowdyn), John, 4, 26, 30;
Sir John, 16; Margery, 2, 4(2);
Richard, 61; William, 3; —, 4
Bowerman (Bowreman), Martin, 65, 68,
74
Bowforest see Beauforest
Bowgher, Harry, 26
Bowhay (Bowhaye), Geraint, 58; Reg-
inald, 2
Bownsham, William, 26
Bowreman see Bowerman
Bowryng, Thomas, 2(2)
Bowth, William, 31
Boyle, Thomas, 41
Brabon, John, 3
Bradbridge, William, bishop of Exeter,
61
Bradmore (Brodmer), John, 20(2), 21,
27, 35, 39
Bragge, Richard, 16
Brailey, William, 69
Bray, Richard, 24
Brayynford, Thomas, 31
Bregan (Bregyn), Philip, 29, 40
Bregard, Oliver, 42
Bregyn see Bregan
Bremelcomb (Bremylcomb), Thomas,
12; —, 12
Brend, James, 53; John, 52
Brenden see Brendon
Brendley, Richard, 76
Brendon (Bendon, Brenden), Richard,
36, 40; Robert, 2
Brereton see Bruerton
Brerewode, Thomas, 17
Bresse, Robert, 40
Breton (Bretyn, Bryttyn), John, 35; John
the, 56; Oliver, 40
Brewartone see Bruerton
Brewer (Bruer), James, 37; Thomas, 29;
William, 68
Brewton, George, 54
see also Bruerton
Brewyster, Henry, 35

Brian (Bryan), John, 3, 45
Bricknoll (Bricknall, Bryckenall, Bryck-
enoll, Brycknoll), Christine, 59, 62;
John, 18, 20, 27, 35, 38, 50; Richard,
68; Thomas, 68; William, 55
Bridgeman (Brigeman, Briggeman,
Brydgeman, Brydgman, Brygeman,
Bryggeman, Brygman, Byrgeman),
Alice, xiiin, 42, 46, 79; Edward, 42, 46,
55; Jasper, 70, 74; John, xii, xiii, xiv,
15, 16, 22, 25(2); Michael, 61; Robert,
12(2), 47; Thomas, 64, 71
Brigge, William, 39
Briggeman see Bridgeman
Brina, Brine see Bryna
Brocadon, James, 68
Brocke, Robert, 75
Brodley see Bodley
Brodmer see Bradmore
Brogyn, John, 52
Broke see Brooke
Brokyn, Richard, 40
Bromefyld, Robert, 52
Brooke (Broke), John, 36, 51, 67; ... tro,
3
Brooks, John, 62
Brounscomb, Roger, 4
Brow, Robert, 2
Browghton, John, 3
Browne, Hugh, 48; John, 1, 13, 24, 37,
51; Michael, 47, 55; Robert, 35;
Roger, 29; Thomas, 20; William, 8,
25, 26(2), 41
Brownemede (Brownemed), Richard, 13,
37
Bruer see Brewer
Bruerton (Brereton, Brewartone, Bruar-
ton), John, 74; Thomas, 61(2), 62,
67(3)
see also Brewton
Brugge, William, 20
Brukcha, Sir John, 21
Brushford, John, 69
Brute, Robert, 55
Bruton, William, 63, 67
Bryan see Brian
Bryant (Bryantt), John, 55; Robert, 47
Bryckenall, Bryckenoll, Brycknall, Bryck-
noll see Bricknoll
Bryddellyngton, John, 2
Brydgeman, Brydgman see Bridgeman
Brygan, Andrew, 11
Brygeman, Bryggeman see Bridgeman
Brygges, William, 14
Brygman see Bridgeman
Brymsdon, John, 3
Bryna (Brina, Brine), Francis, 62, 70, 73
Bryndon, John, 9; Richard, 23
Brysse, Christopher, 29
Bryttell, Richard, 47
Bryttyn see Breton
Buckenham (Bokyngham, Bucknam,
Bucknan, Buckyngham), John, 1, 3;
Margaret, 19(2), 38; William, 19(2),
38, 50, 57
Bucker', William, 12
Buckeram (Bocram, Bokeram, Buckram),
Agnes, 41; John, 26(2); Nicholas, 48;
Robert, 2

Cheney (Cheyney), *Awen*, 20; Thomas, 46
Chepman, George, 3
Cheryte, Edmund, 24; John, 44
Cheryton, John, 13, 14, 42, 46, 50
Chesterton, Robert, 46
Cheswysse, Thomas, 32
Cheyney *see* Cheney
Chicke, Edward, 65, 68, 74
Cholayshe, Anthony, 48; Roger, 45
Cholmore *see* Chalmore
Cholwayt, Michael, 40
Christopher, Richard, 64
Chubb (Chubbe), Matthew, 4; Richard, 13(5), 37; Robert, 2(8); . . .*rt*, 4
Chucheley *see* Chechylley
Chudley (Chuddeley, Chudlegh), James, 3(3), 17; Johane, 24; *Maistras*, 17
Church, William, 48
Claissh (Claysche), John, 4, 16
Clarke (Clark, Clerk, Clerke), Adam, 15; Alnot, 29; Henry, 3, 15, 42, 46; John, 35; Richard, 3, 8; Thomas, 42; William, 28, 35, 55; · · ·, 3
Classe, Edward, 52
Clavell, John, 68, 76
Claw (Clew), Stephen, 1, 2
Claynger *see* Cleyhanger
Claysch *see* Claissh
Cleff *see* Clyff
Clement (Clemente), Edward, 76; John, 36; William, 74
Clerk, Clerke *see* Clarke
Clevehanger, John, 16(2), 48; Robert, 79
see also Cleyhanger
Cleveland (Clevelande), Henry, 64, 69; Johane, 74
Clew *see* Claw
Cleyhanger (Claynger, Cleynger), John, 15; Richard, 26, 41; William, 4
see also Clevehanger
Cleypytt, William, 28
Clyff (Cleff), James, 46; John, 31, 57; Richard, 1(3), 3; William, 40
Clyfton, John, 1, 2
Coake *see* Cook
Cobaton, John, 49
Cobley (Cobleghe), Matthew, 36, 52
Coblond (Coblonde), Robert, 48; William, 15, 42
Cock (Cocke), Hugh, 25; Walter, 31
Cockehyll, John, 40
Code, Robert, 2
Codlyn (Codleyn), Ivan, 38; Iwen, 19
Coffyn, Martin, 8; Matthew, 49
Coke *see* Cook
Coker (Colker), John, 36, 45
Cokeram, Thomas, 35
Colchett, Giles, 4(2); John, 4
Cole (Coley, Coll, Colle), John, 2, 4(2), 5(2), 23, 43, 45; Nicholas, 4; Thomas, 51
Coleton (Collyton, Colton), Edmund, 49; Henry 21; John, 29, 40; Margaret, 49; Peter, 55
Coley *see* Cole
Colford, John, 53
Colker *see* Coker
Coll, Colle *see* Cole

Collen *see* Colyn
Colles (Colls, Collys), Hugh, 12; Humphrey, 12; John, 49; Robert, 74
Collescote (Collscott), Richard, 67, 76
Collins (Collyns), John, 63, 69, 76; Thomas, 51; William, 51
Collscott *see* Collescote
Collyns *see* Collins
Collys *see* Colles
Collyton *see* Coleton
Colman, Anthony, 51; John, 35
Coloff, William, 8(2), 36
Colshull (Colsshull), John, 1(2), 2, 5(2)
Colston, Robert, 50
Colswyll, William, 11
Colter, Roger, 43
Colton *see* Coleton
Colwill (Colwyll), Hubert, 58, 62; Michael, 69; Richard, 25, 41, 53
Colyn (Collen, Colyng), Henry, 17, 30; Neil, 26, 27, 41; Nigel, 25; Paul Faunte, 18; Richard, 40; William, 19; . . .,3(2)
Comb (Come), Elizabeth, 56; Henry, 54, John, 79; Robert, 22
Comyng (Comyn, Coomyn), William, 18, 38, 48, 70
Comysherd, Christopher, 58
Condet, Robert, 37
Coner, Richard, 33
Conet, John, 35
Convers, John, 70, 73
Cooke (Coake, Coakes, Coke, Coocke, Coockes, Cookes), Edmund, 75; Edward, 64, 70; Elizabeth, 46; Henry, 42; John, 3, 31, 45, 48; Oliver, 70, 73; Richard, 7(2), 36; Robert, 43; Thomas, 16, 47, 76; William, 31, 51
Coomyn *see* Comyng
Cooper (Coper, Couper), John, 54, 65, 71, 73, 79; Thomas, 23; William, 13, 42, 54, 59
Copelston, Henry, 17
Coper *see* Cooper
Copp (Coppe), Agnes, 26, 41; *Anys*, 27; Nicholas, 26, 27, 41
Corant, William, 35
Cornelis, . . ., 3
Cornyshe (Cornyssh, Cornysshe), Elizabeth, 3; John, 42, 46; Thomas, 48
Corsett (Corsey), Thomas, 11, 16
Coryer, John, 2
Cosyn, John, 4, 23; Peter, 8, 36; Robert, 13; William, 2, 5, 17, 26, 49
Cote *see* Coty
Coteler, Thomas, 2, 5
Coterell, Margaret, 4; Thomas, 1
Cotoner *see* Cottener
Cotte *see* Coty
Cottener (Cotoner, Cottyner, Cotyner), Robert, 22, 39; Thomas, 16; William, 9, 10(3)
Cottey *see* Coty
Cotton (Cotten, Cottyn, Cutten), Alice, 45; Richard, 31, 37; Robert, 18, 50, 56; Thomas, 18, 42; William, 53, 58; Wilmot, 46
Cottyford *see* Cotyford
Cottyn *see* Cotton